THE SUNDAY TIMES

Write
That Letter!

SECOND EDITION

Iain Maitland

 KOGAN PAGE | *CREATING SUCCESS*

To Tracey, Michael, Sophie and Adam

First published in 1997
Second edition 2000
Reprinted 2004

Kogan Page Limited
120 Pentonville Road
London N1 9JN

www.kogan-page.co.uk

British Library Cataloguing in Publication Data

A CIP record for this book is available from the British Library.

ISBN 0 7494 3253 5

Typeset by Jean Cussons Typesetting, Diss, Norfolk
Printed and bound in Great Britain by Clays Ltd, St Ives plc

contents

introduction

Write That Letter! makes it easier and quicker for you to write business and personal letters. It is ideal if you have to write letters regularly and are not always sure what to put or how to phrase something. With the help of 100 example letters and explanatory comments, this book shows you what to write, and why.

Chapter 1 sets out the secrets of successful letters. Whatever you write, you can now plan each letter properly, and choose the most suitable appearance, layout, format and style for every occasion.

Chapters 2–8 look at 100 of the trickiest letters you're ever likely to have to write, including how to:

- sell to unknown sales leads;
- handle angry customers;
- buy goods at the best prices;
- chase outstanding debts;
- discipline staff; and even
- commiserate with someone who's lost their job.

The easiest and quickest way to write a letter is to check the contents list on pages iii–v, refer to the type of letter you have to write, and read the example and explanatory comments.

This gives you all you need to know. For the fullest understanding of writing letters, you can read the book from cover to cover in the usual way. It's up to you. Whatever you do, you're about to learn the winning tactics for writing difficult letters.

Iain Maitland

the secrets of successful letters

Before you write a sales letter to a prospective customer, a warning letter to a member of staff or any other particularly tricky letter, you need to know how to put difficult letters together properly. You must be able to plan a letter, create the correct appearance for it, choose an appropriate layout, pick a relevant format and select a suitable writing style.

planning your letter

Whether you have to compose a thank-you note or a notice of redundancy, you should plan out what you want to say to the reader, before you put anything down in writing. To prepare properly, you must consider your aims, all the facts and the person who is going to receive your correspondence. With this information to hand, you can then sketch out a rough draft of this difficult letter.

your aims

Begin by contemplating exactly why you are writing this particular letter and what you wish to achieve with it. Perhaps you have to reject a customer's request for a discount, but also want to retain their goodwill and maintain future orders. Maybe you need to remind someone about an unfulfilled promise, encouraging them to fulfil it now. Write out these aims so that they are clear to you when you start writing. They provide a focus for your letter.

the facts

List all the relevant facts relating to the letter. For example, if you are responding to a letter of complaint from a customer, you should be aware of the nature of the complaint, whether or not it is valid, who is responsible if it is valid, and the actions that need to be taken to satisfy the customer. To make sure that you are fully conversant and up to date with the facts, you may need to check your records, look at correspondence and notes of telephone conversations, and take advice, as necessary. As an example, if you are about to dismiss someone, you must always seek legal advice before you do so.

your reader

You need to understand the person who will open your letter as well as you can. Imagine what they will be thinking as they unfold the letter, and work out what it is they want to know and read about. 'What's in it for me?' is a thought that occurs to most readers (albeit sometimes subconsciously). Decide what will make them respond in the way that you want them to do, to submit the next order or pay that outstanding bill. Work out what will trigger the response you want from them.

the rough draft

Having considered your aims, the facts and the person you are writing to, you should be able to put together a rough draft. As an example, imagine that you want to complain about a faulty item that you purchased from a supplier and that is now out of guarantee. Your aims are to obtain a replacement *and* to remain on friendly terms with the supplier as you need to do business with them in the future. You know and have made notes about when you bought the item, the problems you have had, how they were resolved (or not), what has gone wrong now, and how you want this to be dealt with. The person you are addressing is rather dour and matter-of-fact.

Based on this understanding, you can start to list the points that you want to include in the letter – why you are writing, what you bought and when, the problems and their responses, the latest problem, what you want them to do, and by when. Put these points into a draft so that you can work on its appearance, layout, format and style, and eventually produce a final, polished version, ready to be sent to the recipient in due course.

creating the correct appearance

You should consider what your letter should look like when it is forwarded to the customer, supplier, employee or whoever. Of course, if you work for a large company, you may not be able to exert any influence over its appearance at all – typically, you simply dictate what you want to write, it is typed up, you sign the letter, and that's that! If you do have a choice, though, you should select envelopes and paper with some care, think about how the text should appear, and even keep a supply of cards handy for special occasions of a personal nature. These all have an effect on the way in which the letter is received and responded to.

the envelopes

If you have a choice, you should choose top-quality envelopes, which create a professional and classy image. Whites, creams, greys and other discreet colours can help to build on this impression, and may distinguish your letter from those that are sent in standard buff envelopes. Type or print the recipient's name, job title, address and postcode across the centre of the front of the envelope. If you have a rubber-stamp of your firm's name, logo or slogan, print this towards the top left or centre of the front of the envelope, as preferred. Place a first-class stamp in the top right corner – second-class stamps smack of indifference.

the paper

Ideally, choose watermarked, A4-sized paper (297 × 210 centimetres) for longer business letters, and half-sized A5 paper for shorter ones and personal notes in which you thank people, offer sympathy, condolences and the like. Make sure that the paper matches the envelopes selected, and that they fit together properly – use smaller envelopes for A5 sheets of paper. This creates a co-ordinated impression on the reader. When appropriate, it is also a good idea to fold A4 sheets into a third and third again rather than half and then another half. This ensures that the letter will be less creased and thus more attractive and easy to read when it is taken out of the envelope.

the text

A typed letter is essential on most formal occasions, especially when you are representing the firm, for ordering goods, dealing with customers, and so on. A handwritten letter is preferable though when you are writing in a personal capacity or are handling a delicate matter on behalf of the company – for example, extending condolences to someone on the death of their partner.

cards

You will find it useful to keep a range of small, nondescript cards in stock, with illustrations of views, flowers and other inoffensive items on the front and blank insides so that you can add your own message. There will be occasions when you have to thank or congratulate someone, sympathise or offer condolences, and a pleasant card with a personalised message is often more appropriate than a formal letter.

choosing an appropriate layout

Whatever information has to be put into your letter, it will usually need to be set out in a standardised, professional way – unless it is of a personal nature, in which case these guidelines can be relaxed. Generally, a business letter comprises various component parts set down in the same basic order and manner.

the letterhead

A business-like letterhead should be at the top left, centre or right of the paper, as preferred. It should incorporate the firm's name, address, telephone and facsimile numbers, Website or e-mail address, logo and/or slogan, as appropriate.

references

If you deal with large volumes of letters, you may find it helpful to include the recipient's reference number. Usually, the reference will be based on the initials of the writer's and typist's names, the recipient's account number, or something similar. Put 'Your ref' if the recipient has used one in earlier correspondence on the same subject. References should be placed some three to five lines under the letterhead, and a line apart.

the date

Set out the date in full – for example, 7 April 2000 is the norm in the United Kingdom, whereas April 7 2000 is used in the United States and some other countries. Avoid abbreviations such as 'Apr', '7-4-00' and '7/4/2000', which look sloppy and rushed. The date should be put two to three lines below the previous entry.

the reader's details

Next, include the recipient's name, job title (as relevant) and their address – check the spellings as and when necessary, as mis-spelt names can irritate or offend, while an incorrect address or postcode might delay the letter or even lead to it going astray. The reader's details should be incorporated two to three lines beneath the date.

the greeting

The recipient's first name should be used if you know them well and are on good and equal terms with them; if you are not familiar with them, use their last name. Avoid the 'Dear Sir/ Dear Madam' approach, which sounds half-hearted and disinterested. Put the greeting two to three lines underneath the preceding entry.

subject heading

If the letter deals with just one key topic, you may wish to put

'Re: invoice 34' or whatever, in ordinary type, underlined or in capitals at the beginning. This can help to focus the reader's attention straight away. If you do include this, put it one line below the greeting.

the main text

Your text should look neat and easy to read to encourage the recipient to keep reading. Make your paragraphs similar sizes where possible, each dealing with one major point. Incorporate generous margins at the top, sides and bottom of the page to avoid a cramped, unattractive look. The first paragraph should be one line beneath the previous entry, with one line of space between successive paragraphs.

If the letter has to continue on to another page, use a plain (rather than a letterheaded) second sheet. Leave six lines from the top, put the page number, date and the reader's name one after the other down the left-hand margin. Then leave a further two to three lines and start the next paragraph.

the complimentary close

End your letter 'Yours sincerely' if you began with 'Dear Oona', 'Dear Mr Heath', or whatever; 'Yours faithfully' is used only if you started with 'Dear Sir', or something similar (which you should not!). On occasions, less formal conclusions could be included instead: 'All the best', 'With good wishes' and 'Kind regards' are popular alternatives. Place this one line beneath your main text.

the writer's details

Leave five or six lines after the complimentary close and add a clear and sensible signature in that space. A squiggle implies that you are too busy and disinterested in the letter. An elaborate signature indicates pomposity and self-importance. Then type or write your name, stating your job title one line under that, if appropriate.

other entries

If you attach something to the letter or enclose anything else in the envelope, you should put 'enclosure', 'enclosures', 'enc' or 'encs' (as appropriate) two lines below the last entry. Similarly, if a copy (or copies) of the letter has been sent elsewhere, you would add 'Copy: Tim Reed' or whatever, two lines beneath the previous entry.

picking a format

There are various ways in which the component parts of a business letter can be laid out on the page – you may be expected to adhere to your company's preferred format or you could be able to pick your own. The three main formats are as follows.

blocked format

With this format, all the entries are placed against an invisible, left-hand margin. This is by far the most popular format in use nowadays.

semi-blocked format

Here, any references included in the letter are set against the invisible right-hand margin, along with the date. They are placed in this position for filing and reference purposes.

indented format

The indented format may follow the same layout as either the blocked or semi-blocked formats, but will differ in that the paragraphs will each be indented by five or six spaces.

selecting your writing style

Having sketched out a rough draft and worked on its appearance, layout and format, you can go on to think about language, tone and length, before producing the final, polished version.

language

Your language should match the knowledge and understanding of the reader, whom you will have considered carefully when you started planning the letter. Use simple words when writing to a member of the public; they may feel confused or alienated by technical phrases, for example. Likewise, employ trade expressions when addressing informed associates, as they might feel patronised by over-simplified language. Always avoid personal slang, in-house jargon and local expressions, as these are rarely understood universally.

tone

If it is to be studied carefully, your letter should have some style – it should not be read as if it is just another standardised circular, churned out along with hundreds of others (even if it is!). Its tone should reflect your personality, that of the recipient and the nature of the letter. Try to write naturally using your own words, using 'please', 'thank you' and even 'sorry', as appropriate. Be mindful of what the reader is like – as a general rule, steer clear of humour unless you know them extremely well and are convinced that they will be amused. Sound sincere and be aware of the seriousness of the situation, or whatever is appropriate.

length

Regardless of the subject, your letter should always be brief and to the point. As an example, the recipient wants to learn how and when you are going to deal with the damaged goods that have been delivered to them, rather than receive a long and detailed explanation of how the damage happened. Keep those aims in mind at all times. Eliminate all superfluous and repetitive comments. Say what you have to state and no more.

the final version

Once you have pulled all this information together and produced the polished version of your letter, you should check it carefully for any spelling, punctuation or grammatical errors. Mistakes, however minor, reflect badly on your standards of professionalism and competence, and could even be misleading if figures are involved. If you see anything wrong with the letter or the envelope, redo it. If in doubt, give it to someone else as a double-check. It is surprising how many mistakes are spotted by other people. It's often difficult to see your own errors, even if they're staring you straight in the face! Submit it only when it is perfect and you are totally satisfied with it in every way.

winning tactics: a step-by-step checklist

1. Know your aims. These provide a direction for your letter.

2. Be aware of all the facts – never write anything until you do.

3. Understand the reader and in particular what they want to know. 'What's in it for me?' is their primary concern. This is more important than what you wish to tell them!

4. Always compose a rough draft, which can then be amended and polished, as necessary.

5. Use good quality paper and envelopes, and make sure that they match each other.

6. Type or write, according to the circumstances. A hand-written note is often more appropriate in personal or delicate situations, perhaps when someone is ill or has died.

7. Send a card rather than a letter, if it feels right to do so.

8. Use these entries as the framework of your letter – letter-head, references, date, reader's details, greeting, subject heading, main text, complimentary close, writer's details and any other entries, as relevant.

9. Choose a format that suits you, whether blocked, semi-blocked or indented. Blocked is universally most popular.

10. Use language that matches the knowledge and under-standing of the recipient. If in doubt, keep it clear and simple.

11. Give the letter some style – it is a unique letter written for a particular reader and no one else. Use your own words and phrases whenever you can.

12. Make certain that the letter is as brief and as direct as possible, deleting any repetition or waffle.

13. Always check the final version carefully for mistakes, rewritting the letter or envelope, as necessary. Get a second opinion.

14. Send that winning business letter!

making sales

Sales letters are among the most difficult to write, simply because you are usually trying to obtain something from a (potentially disinterested) person or business – almost inevitably, it is an order! Often, a sales letter will be sent under the guise of an introduction to your firm, or to new or revamped products. On other occasions, these letters will need to defend a difficult position, while still attempting to persuade people and organisations to keep buying – in spite of amended trading terms or increased prices, a delayed order or a rejected request for a discount. Maybe a customer has not placed an order for some time and needs to be contacted to find out why and, if possible, to remedy the situation.

introducing your firm

Dear Mr McGann

We write to introduce ourselves to you as a business that provides computer sales, consultancy and maintenance services to growing companies in the South-East of England. Our clients include Hansens, Pargetter Smith and K D Little.

In particular, we offer:

- ■ Purpose-built computer systems and software to meet a company's exact requirements.
- ■ Consultancy services, including one-day training seminars for managers and employees involved with operating computer systems and software.
- ■ Same-day service contracts for organisations within a 50-mile radius of our offices.

At this stage, we enclose our latest brochure for your perusal. If you are interested in our range of products and services either now or in the future, please call me on my direct line – 01219 348293. We would be pleased to supply further details on request or to discuss your requirements, without obligation.

We look forward to your call.

Yours sincerely

Leon Astle
Sales Manager

---

comments

1. This is a tricky letter to write because you are trying to sell your firm and its products and services to a prospective customer – and potentially, someone who has not heard of you. It is comparable to a cold-call telephone conversation and just as difficult to do well.
2. In the opening paragraph, introduce your firm, goods and services but in very broad terms in order to attract and maintain the widest possible interest. If you are

too specific, some recipients may stop reading straight away as they might conclude that this is not for them. Obviously, you must make them read on so that they are encouraged to find out more, thus giving you the chance to sell to them. Establish your credibility by referring to clients whom the reader will either know personally or will have heard of and respects.

3. Provide succinct, general comments about what your firm has to offer, perhaps in an easy-to-read bullet-point format, as shown in the sample letter. Again, you do not want to be too detailed at this stage as precise references to prices, terms, conditions and the like will answer the recipient's questions and may enable them to stop reading. Keep them interested and (better still) curious to learn more – to discover what is in it for them!

4. In the concluding paragraph, you might wish to refer to any accompanying literature enclosed with the letter, and then encourage the recipient to get in touch with you. Giving your telephone number makes this easy for them and more likely that they will respond. Indicate that any discussions will be without obligation – again, another encouragement. If, or when, they telephone, you will be well on the way to success and can go on to establish a trading relationship with them.

requesting an introduction

Dear Steve

I wonder if you could do me a favour? I am going to be in Ipstone on Monday 18 November and would like to meet Danny Davies at Hoppers. Could you give him a call to introduce me?

I think Danny may be interested in the new range of picture frames we are producing and I would welcome the opportunity to show these to him. I am sure that an introduction by you would increase my chances of arranging a meeting.

If you could call him in the next week or so, I would be extremely grateful as this will then enable me to set up a meeting in time for Monday 18 November. Many thanks indeed.

All good wishes to you.

Yours sincerely

Ross Carne

comments

1. This type of letter can only be written if both you and the recipient know the intermediary very well and respect that person. Also, the recipient must be willing to act as a go-between for you, so they will need to feel extremely confident in your ability to fulfil expectations. Do not write a letter of this kind unless these criteria are met, otherwise you cannot hope to succeed.
2. The first paragraph has to make it clear exactly what you want from them – be direct rather than circumspect, which is embarrassing and potentially confusing.
3. It is sensible to follow this with a brief explanation of how the introduction will benefit the recipient and you. As you will know the prospective intermediary well, you should not need to say what is in it for them – they should be happy to recommend you because it is good business practice to help each other whenever possible. Adding something to the effect of 'if you do

this for me, I'll do that for you' sounds like a clumsy bribe and may cause offence.

4. Your final paragraph should reiterate what you want the recipient to do and by when, as appropriate. Even though it is tempting to be vague and hopeful because you are asking a favour, it is better to be specific so that they know what they have to do.

5. Make this letter very friendly and informal, addressing the recipient by their first name, using positive and upbeat language and thanking them when relevant, but not profusely. A handwritten letter may be more effective than a formal typed one, if you know them very well indeed.

offering new products

Dear Mrs Joyce

We are pleased to introduce you to the latest addition to our fast-expanding range of baby transporters – the Wayliner.

This innovative product is a twin pushchair, with three distinctive features:

■ A revolutionary 'twist and ride' seat – you can change baby's seat position with a flick of the wrist.
■ An all-new, chip-resistant white frame, especially easy for cleaning off grubby fingermarks.
■ Fixings for an additional seat to be added – making it easy for an older child to ride along.

For a very limited period, we are making a special offer available exclusively to our customers:

■ A 10 per cent discount off the normal trade price of each pushchair.

- A free sun-shade or rain-cover with every pushchair.
- A free rotating sales-display unit for each customer who places an order for 12 pushchairs or more.

We enclose sales literature for the Wayliner. To take advantage of the offer, call our 24-hour Wayliner Hotline on 01800 800980. Please note that this offer is for a very limited period.

We look forward to receiving your call.

Yours sincerely

Derek Padbury
Sales Manager

---

comments

1. Typically, this letter will be written for and sent to existing or prospective customers who know your firm, goods and services well, and think favourably of them. Thus, you will have their goodwill and can feel more confident that they will at least read your letter to the end. You should adhere to a basic framework when writing it.

2. Compose a simple and straightforward letter: introduce the new product or service as appropriate, specify those features that distinguish it from other, comparable goods available, explain what is in it for the reader and encourage them to place an order by making it easy for them to contact you. Pressurise them gently into doing so by indicating that the offer is for a limited period or that stocks are low, or something similar.

3. If you want to write and announce the availability of new products to someone who is not familiar with what you have to offer, you may prefer to compose more of an introductory letter that encourages the recipient to contact you to find out more about them, as illustrated in the letter on page 14.

announcing revamped products

Dear Mervyn

We are absolutely delighted to be able to announce an exciting new development in our range of products and services. The ever-popular Biarritz suite has been upgraded to meet changing customer requirements.

All new features include:

■ A choice of three colours – peach, mustard or mint.
■ Reversible cushions incorporating two designs – stripes and checks. Two looks in one suite!
■ Removable covers – for easy cleaning!

Its most popular features remain the same:

■ A luxury flat-weave fabric.
■ Cigar-shaped arms with deep, fibre-filled back and seat cushions, and fully sprung seats.
■ Frames mounted on castors for maximum manoeuvrability.
■ Four co-ordinating scatter cushions included free of charge.

All this, and for just £899 plus VAT – the same price as before!

New sales literature is enclosed for your attention. We are taking orders for the updated version now, for deliveries commencing 1 October. Orders will be processed on an 'as received' basis and despatched in the same way. Please note that initial stocks are very limited, so place your order now by calling our sales team on 01992 930343.

We look forward to hearing from you.

Yours sincerely

Tom Hebbs
Manager

---

comments

1. Announcing that a product or service has been improved is always a difficult task. Inevitably, you will have praised the original version, so to revamp it subsequently may indicate that perhaps it was not quite as good as you had claimed. This can create disappointment and even some resentment between your customers and you, unless the situation is handled well.

2. Probably the best approach is to suggest that the original product was good, but that you have listened to customers' comments and have now made it even better as a result of their suggestions.

3. Your letter should begin by making this point. Then specify the main, new features and how they will benefit the recipient. Follow this by setting out the features that remain unchanged, which readers may find re-assuring. End by referring to the enclosed sales literature and encouraging the recipient to order, typically by providing a telephone number and indicating that they need to act fast because stocks are limited or whatever.

chasing a reluctant buyer

Dear Mr Tonkinson

We were delighted to receive your enquiry about the Prima Donna early last month and to send our agent, Kiefer Lodge, to demonstrate it for you in your home. We are sure you were impressed with it.

We can confirm that this produce is still available on the same terms that were offered by Kiefer when you met – £799.95, paid over 12 months on an interest-free basis. We have the Prima Donna that you wanted in stock for immediate delivery.

However, this is a limited offer and is due to close at the end of this month when stocks are expected to be exhausted. We would be happy to put one aside for you, though, on request.

I am pleased to enclose our sales literature for your perusal. For further information, please do not hesitate to call me on my direct line – 01777 717476. Alternatively, Kiefer can be contacted on his mobile on 0793 1619393.

We look forward to hearing from you again.

Our best wishes

Laurie Kirkup
Sales Director

comments

1. Inevitably, there will be some customers who need to be chased before they make a purchase, but this has to be done carefully and diplomatically if they are to go

on to buy from you. This letter is difficult to write –
you have to tread a difficult line, pushing enough to
generate a response, but not so much that you alienate
them and lose their custom.

2. The initial paragraph has to open the letter in a very
positive and upbeat way, perhaps by referring to their
provisional enquiry and how you responded to it.
Never reproach the customer for not having followed
through with a firm order. There should no hint of
recrimination at all, as this will only offend them and
reduce your chances of a sale.

3. Next, you must re-establish their interest by telling
them about the product again, and reminding them
what is in it for them – interest-free credit and immediate delivery in this example.

4. Worry them a little in the following paragraph by
stating that this is a limited offer – prices may rise,
stocks could sell out, or whatever. You want them to
respond quickly to your letter and this can be a good
way of achieving it.

5. The last paragraph has to give them a chance to reply
now and secure this uncertain sale, so provide telephone numbers, an order form and envelope, or whatever is appropriate in your situation.

announcing amended trading terms

Dear Mr Chaplin

We write to advise you of our terms of trade as from 1 April. The
main terms are as follows:

■ Payment with order discount – 5 per cent off list prices.
■ Payment within seven days of receipt of invoice – a 3.5 per
cent discount may be deducted by customers.

- ■ Payment within 30 days of receipt of invoice – a 2 per cent discount may be deducted by customers.
- ■ Credit terms for authorised customers – strictly, payment by the end of the month following the month of receipt of the invoice.
- ■ Further orders will not be processed on those accounts where outstanding balances are overdue for payment.
- ■ Goods to be returned for credit to customer's accounts will be at our discretion.

Should you have any queries about your account, please do not hesitate to call me on 01796 116164.

With best wishes

Your sincerely

Barry Hutchinson
Sales Manager

---

comments

1. The problem with this type of letter is that you are almost certainly passing on unfavourable news – prompt or bulk-buy discounts are being trimmed, credit terms shortened, and the like. As a consequence, customers are more likely to take their trade elsewhere, unless you can write an effective letter.

2. You can approach this letter in one of two ways. There is a strong argument to suggest that you should simply list all your main terms of trade – both changed and unchanged – without drawing attention to the

amended ones, in case this sounds negative and defensive. Sending what appears to be a routine, standardised circular can be appropriate if the changes are not too significant, the unchanged terms are generally good – it can be a wise move to make one or two minor but positive adjustments to these – and the reader is given the opportunity to contact you if they have any queries.

3. Alternatively, you can tackle a major, adverse change to trading terms head on in the same basic way that you would write the following letter explaining price rises. Obviously, the approach that you will take will depend on your individual circumstances.

explaining price rises

Dear Geoff

We write to tell you that we will be increasing the prices of our product range by 4 per cent from 1 January. This is our first price rise in three years but is now unavoidable because of the increased costs of raw materials and component parts during this time.

Our products will continue to be made to the same high standards and will still represent outstanding value for money in the marketplace. Our new catalogue is enclosed to remind you of all our products, which are at very competitive prices and are all available for immediate despatch.

Finally, as a special offer to our valued customers, we can confirm that our prices remain at current rates for all goods ordered prior to 31 December, regardless of when you want them to be delivered. Goods will be invoiced as at the date of delivery.

An order form is enclosed for your convenience, along with a stamped addressed envelope.

With good wishes

Your sincerely

Terry Osgood
Manager

---

comments

1. Some firms notify customers of imminent price rises in a standardised circular, while others simply raise them without advance notification – either way, ill feeling and confusion can develop as a consequence. Sending a personal letter, albeit often personalised by the careful use of a word processor, may defuse an awkward situation.
2. Key information should be put across in the opening paragraph – in particular, the fact that there is going to be a price increase, how much it will be and when it will take place. Be precise here. Give a reason for the rise, but without making it sound like an excuse. If this is the first increase for some time, say so. This makes it look as though you are on the same side, tackling overseas suppliers, inflation or whatever together.
3. Build on this in the next paragraph by reminding the customer what you have to offer them – high standards, competitive prices, and the like. Show them, too, by enclosing sales literature, and so on.
4. A special offer in the last paragraph – typically, all orders processed at existing prices if received before a certain date – can persuade a customer to place

another order. This can be encouraged further by enclosing an order form and a stamped addressed envelope.

5. It is important that this letter does not have an apologetic tone, but deals with the price rise in a matter-of-fact way and then sweeps aside any concerns by becoming very upbeat and positive. Price rises are a fact of business life and must be treated as such.

acknowledging an unprocessed order

Dear Matthew

We acknowledge receipt of your order 564 of 9 September, which is currently receiving our attention.

We are at present awaiting delivery of component parts from our overseas supplier and expect to receive these in the next seven to ten days. Finished goods will be produced within ten days of this and then despatched to you straight away.

We trust this is agreeable to you. If not, we would be pleased to offer you 12 de luxe AZ6-1-X models as an alternative. In the circumstances, we would be happy to supply these at the same price as the 12 standard AX610-Y models ordered. They are available for immediate despatch.

We look forward to hearing from you.

Best regards

Lizzie Riley
Sales Director

comments

1. There are occasions when a firm is unable to fulfil an order, or at least cannot do so within the usual accepted period of time. Many businesses fail to tell their customers of this, either through apathy, incompetence or the hope that nothing will be said and a late delivery can be made. However, it is far better to let them know and to offer them an alternative if appropriate, than to risk the animosity that is so often created in such circumstances.

2. Begin by acknowledging the order as soon as possible after it has been received. Do respond straight away to show that you are a well-run, caring organisation.

3. Rather than concentrating on your inability to process the order now, focus instead on telling the recipient when it will be dealt with and delivered. Always turn negative news into positive comments, wherever possible. Give firm dates rather than generalisations such as 'in the near future' and 'at the earliest opportunity', because everyone defines these phrases differently. Make sure that the dates given are realistic to avoid further disappointment.

4. If there is a chance that the order might be lost, do suggest alternative goods that can be despatched sooner, and offer them at a reduced price to secure the order, if necessary.

5. Of course, some orders will not be processed because the customer has exceeded their credit limit or has fallen behind with their payments, in which case, a different approach will be required. Letters sent in response to this situation are dealt with in Chapter 5, pages 75, 77 and 80.

rejecting a request for a discount

Dear Ms Patel

Thank you for your letter of 16 October requesting a 10 per cent discount if you purchase goods to the value of £250 from us.

Our policy on discounts is to give 5 per cent on orders exceeding £500, 7.5 per cent above £750 and 10 per cent on those exceeding £1,000. We would be happy to give you a 2.5 per cent discount for an order totalling £250.

However, we also offer a 5 per cent discount on orders paid for on a pro forma or on-collection basis, or 2.5 per cent if settlement is made within 30 days of purchase.

With this in mind, we would be pleased to give you a 6.5 per cent discount if you spent £250 with us and paid on a pro forma or on-collection basis.

We look forward to hearing from you shortly.

Yours sincerely

Pat Buchan
Manager

comments

1. Increasingly, firms are asking for discounts on relatively modest orders and it is tempting to dismiss these automatically. Nevertheless, it is often worth trying to see if a compromise can be reached, especially if they are new and potentially long-term

customers. At the same time, you need to be careful not to set an unreasonable precedent for future dealings, nor to run the risk of alienating existing customers who do not receive any discounts of note.

2. In the initial paragraph, it is useful to set out the offer but without commenting on or rejecting it outright, as this may sound rather dismissive.

3. Moving on, you should specify what you normally provide in terms of discounts and make a counter offer based on this.

4. You may want to add to this in a third paragraph, perhaps offering a one-off, first-time buyer's discount or, more likely, a discount that is linked to pro forma or on-collection delivery payment. This is more sensible as it increases the discount available, secures payment from a new and unknown customer and avoids offending other customers who may object to discounts they are not receiving.

5. Conclude this polite but brisk letter by putting the onus on the recipient to respond – 'we look forward to your response', or something similar.

enquiring about loss of custom

Dear Kulvinder

As we have not heard from you for some time, we thought we would write to keep you up to date on developments here at Gayfer & Sons Ltd. Since we last supplied goods to you, we have:

- ■ Introduced a new line of Scandinavian furnishings and accessories that may be of particular interest to you.
- ■ Increased our product range by more than 20 per cent, and it continues to expand.

■ Maintained prices at the same levels. These will remain the same for the foreseeable future.

We also continue to offer the same benefits to our customers as before:

■ Immediate despatch from stocks.
■ 48-hour guaranteed delivery and at no extra cost to you.
■ 5 per cent discount for payment with order or a 2.5 per cent discount for payment in 30 days.
■ A no-quibble, money-back guarantee for goods returned within 14 days of receipt.

So why not give us another try? We enclose your latest catalogue, price list and order form for your attention. Should you wish to discuss or view our products, please call our agent, Brenda Holmes, on 01232 7568590. For other queries, please contact me on 01980 564738, extension 248.

With our best wishes

Yours

Matt Fischer
Manager

---

comments

1. It is helpful if this letter can immediately establish as close a relationship with the recipient as possible – the use of their first name may achieve this.
2. The first paragraph should show interest, but without reproof or suggesting that there is a problem.
3. The bulk of the letter must then concentrate on positive issues and what the firm can offer the recipient,

rather than focus on problems as so many of these types of letter do. Using bullet points can help to put across this information in a succinct, easy-to-absorb way.

4. The concluding paragraph should encourage the reader to get in touch, either to discuss an unstated problem or, more likely, to place an order. Including telephone numbers is often a good idea.

caring for customers

Some customer care letters should be relatively simple to compose if you adhere to a basic framework – for example, thank you's for first, large and continued orders. Others are more difficult to write, usually because you have to deal with an angry and complaining customer who is dissatisfied with your products or the service provided. Sometimes you will want to send a letter in anticipation of a complaint – for example, when goods are not available or have been delayed.

thanking a customer for a first order

Dear Mr di Carlo

I write to thank you for placing your first order with us.

By now, you will have received your goods and I trust you are happy with them and the service provided on this occasion. Should you have any queries, do not hesitate to contact me on 01963 280385, extension 666.

While writing, I am pleased to enclose a copy of our new catalogue, price list and order forms. I hope this is the beginning of a long and mutually rewarding association.

With good wishes

Yours sincerely

Dominic Newton
Sales Director

---

comments

1. Some firms write to customers to thank them for their first order. Letters of thanks help to identify any queries or problems, establish an immediate rapport, set the company apart from competitors and, hopefully, create the foundations for a solid, long-term relationship.
2. To begin with, a simple 'thank you' is very effective. Put this in your opening line.
3. In the first, main paragraph, indicate that you trust that they are happy with your goods and services and ask them to telephone you if they have any comments or queries – such a conversation can create good relations between you. Do not use the word 'problems', as many businesses do, as this will cause concern and might even encourage the customer to look for shortcomings where none exist.
4. In the following paragraph, give the customer a reason to place a further order by enclosing a sales catalogue, order form, and the like. You need to build straight away on this initial success. If a response is not forthcoming, you should follow up your letter, perhaps with a telephone call.

5. Conclude in a warm and friendly manner – 'with good wishes' or something similar.
6. It is sensible to send your letter after the goods have been despatched and received by the customer so that any difficulties will have come to light by that time. The best time for your letter to arrive is a few days after the goods have been received.

thanking a customer for a large order

Dear Ms Porter

Many thanks indeed for your order TN17-452, which we received this morning.

This is a substantial order and we have already started processing it for you. It will be given our best attentions and will be delivered to you on 12 September.

All the best

David O'Shea
Distributions Manager

comments

1. There are many ways of building a good business relationship, one of which is to acknowledge a substantial order.
2. To start, thank the customer for their order. Then say that it is a large order and you are already working on it. Finally, state when it will be delivered – the more precise you can be, the better.

3. You must be careful not to create the impression that this is a standardised circular, sent automatically to everyone. Circulars never impress. Personalise it as and when you can – 'all the best', and so on.
4. At the same time, you do not wish to appear excessively grateful, as this can make you seem desperate for business and could encourage the customer to press hard for a discount next time around. A straightforward 'thank you' is sufficient.

thanking a customer for their continued custom

Dear Mariella

I am writing to thank you for your continued custom over the past year. During that time, we have increased our product range by more than half and developed our Express Delivery and Rapid Refund services, which have proved to be extremely popular.

For the coming year, we are planning further developments. Based on customer requests and ongoing research, we are sure that these will be equally welcomed by the trade when they are unveiled at the Spring Fair in Germany on 20–22 March.

Don't forget that we always welcome your views on our goods and services so that we can continue to meet all your stock requirements.

Thank you again for your ongoing custom.

Yours sincerely

Den Sykes
Customer Services Manager

comments

1. In the same way that thanking a customer for their first order and subsequent large ones can help to establish and build relations, thanking them for their past custom at regular, yearly intervals or whenever, can enable you to maintain that successful relationship. Also, it gives you an opportunity to promote your firm, and its products and services for the future.
2. Open by thanking the customer for their custom, which focuses their attention and puts them in a positive frame of mind towards you.
3. Remind them what has happened over the past year or so – in essence, what you have done and achieved for them. Perhaps low prices have been sustained or the range of goods available has been increased.
4. Say what is going to happen over the coming year. Encourage them to keep trading by telling them about your exciting plans for new services, and so forth.
5. Round off the letter by stating that you always welcome their comments, and thank them again for their business.

investigating a complaint

Dear Norris

We are very disappointed to learn of the problems you are having with the Midway that you purchased from us in June. All of our products are subject to the most stringent testing and checking procedures before they are sold and we do not know why these problems have arisen on this occasion.

We are arranging to have the item collected at the earliest opportunity so that we can ascertain the cause of the difficulties and resolve the situation on your behalf. Our Despatch Manager, Stuart Hay, will telephone you shortly to arrange a precise collection time that is convenient to you.

Assuring you of our best attentions,

Yours sincerely

Laurence Cohen
Customer Relations Manager

---

comments

1. When a complaint is made – typically about goods – you do not know whether it is justified or not. A product may be inherently faulty or have been used incorrectly or mistreated. Thus, your initial written response has to be sympathetic, positive and non-committal at the same time, which is difficult to achieve!

2. In the first paragraph, say that you are sorry to hear about the problems they are experiencing, but do not refer to 'faults'. Never commit yourself until you know the exact cause of the difficulty.

3. The second paragraph should set up a defensive position, just in case, by indicating how thoroughly the goods are examined before they are released and that you do not know why the problems have arisen. Be careful not to express surprise or even disbelief here, though, as this will offend a genuine customer.

4. In the third paragraph, state what you are going to do to deal promptly with the matter, making sure that you are able to do whatever you are promising. Be very helpful and positive as you end the letter.

5. If, on inspecting the products, you decide that they are faulty, you can accept the complaint (as below). Alternatively, you may conclude that you want to reject the complaint (see page 40). Either way, do act quickly to resolve the matter. Unsettled complaints tend to become more irritating and annoying to the customer the longer they're unresolved.

accepting a complaint

Dear Mrs Broome

Thank you for your letter of 18 March concerning the TS-500 unit that you bought from us at the end of last year. We have examined the unit and agree that it is faulty. We accept responsibility for this and apologise for it.

As requested, we are arranging for the unit to be replaced. A new model will be delivered to you on Friday 6 April.

Once again, please accept our apologies for this incident.

Yours sincerely

Durvin Sandiford
Customer Liaison Manager

comments

1. This is a difficult letter to write because many managers try to adhere closely to the 'never explain, never apologise' approach. Evidently, this has its merits – you do not want to be seen to make mistakes,

      nor leave yourself open to a claim against you. Nevertheless, there will be occasions when it is clear that a complaint is absolutely justified, and to deny it will only lead to further confrontation and damaged relations.

2. An acceptance of a complaint should follow a set format: acknowledge the situation, agree with the complaint and apologise, go along with their suggested solution if it is reasonable or propose an alternative if it is not, and apologise for the incident again. The tone of the letter needs to be polite but brisk. There was a problem and you have dealt fairly with it – end of story!

rejecting a complaint

Dear Mr Ash

Thank you for your letter of 29 August telling us about the XTW-300A computer that your purchased from us on 19 June. Our service engineer, Liz Thorson, has examined the machine and is unable to find any faults within the system. Therefore, we are not able to provide you with a replacement computer.

However, we would be happy to arrange for our sales consultant, Jim McReadie, to call on you at your convenience to go through the system with you so that you are fully aware of its capabilities. If you would care to call me on 01768 786899, I will make an appointment for you.

Yours sincerely

Mary Tate
Installation Manager

comments

1. Rejecting a customer's complaint is invariably one of the most difficult letters you will have to write, especially if the customer is genuinely convinced that their complaint is justified, and you wish to retain their goodwill and future custom. Typically, a complaint will focus on products and services, as in the example. To maintain a good working relationship, your letter needs to be both polite and diplomatic. This is difficult to achieve when effectively you are refusing to agree with them and what they say.

2. Open by acknowledging their complaint, but without commenting on it one way or the other. Try to avoid confrontational language from the start, referring to 'your comments about...', 'the situation concerning...', or something similar, rather than 'your complaint'.

3. You should reject their complaint in the next paragraph, stating that you can discover nothing wrong with the product, no indication of errors being made by staff, or whatever. Again, be diplomatic – 'we cannot find any flaws' is better than 'there is nothing wrong with it'. One sounds helpful, sympathetic and leaves the way open for further discussion if proof is made available; the other is blunt, dismissive and will cause offence.

4. If you think that the customer is sincere and not simply trying to obtain a replacement for a mistreated or worn-out product, or is being unreasonably demanding about a service, it is a good idea to offer some form of assistance or compromise deal, assuming that this is not too costly and will not set an expensive precedent for the future. Advice on how to make the most of a product or service by using it differently is useful and mutually beneficial, if it reduces complaints in the future.

apologising for an employee's conduct

Dear Miss Peters

Thank you for your letter of 1 December concerning your visit to our premises that morning. We have investigated the incident thoroughly and have disciplined the employee concerned. Please accept our apologies for what happened, and be assured that it will not occur again.

Thank you for drawing this matter to our attention, and for giving us the opportunity to deal with it.

Yours sincerely

Ivan Costello
Branch Manager

comments

1. There will be occasions – hopefully rare ones – when somebody will complain about one of your employee's activities. On investigation, you will conclude that the complaint is a valid criticism. Having disciplined the employee in accordance with company guidelines, you will then need to write to the customer or whoever made the complaint.
2. Make the letter brief and simple. Acknowledge the reason why you are writing, say that you have investigated the incident, have disciplined the employee and that such an incident will not happen again. Conclude by thanking them for drawing the matter to your attention.

3. Be polite and sincere, with 'please' and 'thank you' as and where relevant. At the same time, you do not want to dwell on this issue, so adopt a succinct, professional tone. An incident happened, you were pleased to be told of it, you dealt with it firmly – that's the end of the matter.

apologising for unavailable goods

Dear Dennis

Many thanks for your order 782 of 19 January. We regret to inform you that the SP-12 items requested are no longer being manufactured. However, we can offer you RT-36 models instead and these are ready for immediate despatch.

RT-36s are similar to the old SP-12s, but are slightly longer. Normally, they are available at £79.95 each, but we would be pleased to offer them to you at the SP-12 price of £74.50 on this occasion. A photograph and further details of the RT-36 are enclosed for your attention.

The balance of your order will be despatched on 26 January and will arrive on the following day. Please let us know if you would like us to send the RT-36s to you. They can be despatched at the same time if you wish.

Yours sincerely

Anne Burke
Sales Co-ordinator

comments

1. When an order is received for goods that are no longer made or will be out of stock for some considerable time, it is often put to one side until the increasingly angry and disgruntled customer enquires further. They are then told about the position and consequently take their custom elsewhere, perhaps never to return. However, an order of this kind can be turned into business and good relations maintained, if a prompt and helpful letter is sent upon its receipt.

2. The key to success is to begin by acknowledging the order, explaining the situation straight away, and offering an alternative to the ordered goods. Clearly, these alternatives should be as similar in every respect to the originals as possible if they are to be accepted.

3. Provide concise details of the alternative goods, indicating how they compare to and differ from the original ones. If the differences can be seen to be minimised, so much the better. Maybe you can sell them individually instead of in their normal packs of four, or you can reduce the prices a little. Enclose some additional data about the goods, such as a photograph and/or their specifications.

4. Finish the letter by making encouraging comments – the goods are available for immediate release, and so on. Do not push too hard, though. You should create the impression that you are suggesting these goods to assist them, not you. The final choice is theirs alone.

apologising for delayed goods

Dear Raj

I write to apologise for this delay in delivering your order 43, dated 17 July.

We have had some problems in obtaining imported component parts for our Domino range but are now in the process of changing to a home-based supplier.

Accordingly, we expect to be able to forward your order to you within the next fortnight. Again, please accept my apologies for the inconvenience caused on this occasion.

With good wishes

Yours

Eddie Tudor
Manager

comments

1. Sadly, this type of letter is written infrequently, with many firms preferring simply to deliver goods as and when they can and without comment, even if this happens to be later than usual or expected! To maintain a sound working relationship, you should always tell customers if goods will be delayed significantly and by how long so that they can plan accordingly.
2. You do not need to be too specific or detailed to make this an effective letter. Just apologise for the delay, give the reason without making your apology sound like an

excuse, state when the order will be delivered, and apologise again.

3. Be careful not to write in too apologetic or negative a manner, and never hint at the possibility that they might go elsewhere – if you do, they probably will! If the delay is so significant that they might be tempted to approach another supplier, offer alternatives, on preferential terms if necessary.

apologising for the wrong goods being sent

Dear Ms Birtles

Thank you for your letter of 14 January. I regret to note that we delivered 12 Conway items instead of the 12 Royston units ordered by you. This was an oversight on our part and I apologise for it.

We are now preparing a replacement order, which will be delivered to you on Wednesday morning. We will collect the Conway items at the same time.

Once again, please accept my apologies for this unfortunate error. Procedures have been put in place to ensure that it does not happen in the future.

Yours sincerely

Dorothy Aldred
Customer Care Supervisor

comments

1. Inevitably, the wrong goods will be sent to customers on occasions – although hopefully, these will be kept to a minimum. When such a situation does occur, most customers will want two things from you – an apology and replacements as soon as possible.

2. In your opening paragraph, you should acknowledge what has happened, accept responsibility and apologise for the error. Do not go into the reasons – you do not want to detail any shortcomings in your firm unless you have to, nor is the customer that interested. They are more concerned to know what you are going to do about their complaint.

3. In the second paragraph, tell them what you are doing and be seen to be acting immediately. State when the replacements will be delivered and the other items will be picked up. If there is likely to be a delay of any note, you may have to offer some form of incentive to persuade them not to go elsewhere – retention of the wrong goods free of charge, perhaps, or a discount on their replacements.

4. In the concluding paragraph, apologise once more and indicate that you have taken steps to prevent such an error from happening on other occasions. As before, you do not need to go into any detailed explanation – the customer just wants to be reassured that the problem will not reoccur for them. They are not particularly interested in how you will put the matter right – just that it is put right for them!

apologising for damaged goods being sent

Dear Ms Uhogo

We are very sorry to learn that the goods delivered to you on 7 November were damaged. We believe this must have happened while they were in transit as all items are inspected and checked carefully before they are packed and despatched to our customers.

We are arranging for a duplicate order to be made up and despatched today. This will be with you within 48 hours of despatch. The damaged goods will be collected at the same time and credited back to your account.

Please accept our apologies for this unfortunate incident.

Yours sincerely

Matt Jeffries
Sales Director

comments

1. Most businesses are familiar with the common problem of goods being damaged in transit and receiving notification of this from irate customers once they have removed the items from their packaging. A potentially awkward situation can be averted swiftly with the help of a letter of apology being sent straight away, and appropriate action being taken thereafter.
2. In the opening paragraph, acknowledge what has happened, but without making it sound as though it

has never occurred before (which appears confrontational) or that it happens frequently (which suggests that your firm is incapable of delivering goods properly).

3. You should keep your message simple. Give a reason why the problem occurred, but do not blame anyone. If you blame the carrier, for example, it reflects badly on you. 'Why do you use them, then?' is the obvious response. Indicate that this is one of those unfortunate incidents that arises on odd occasions, and that you're going to put it right.

4. Say what you will do to remedy the situation. Ideally, you should be willing to replace and collect the damaged items at the earliest opportunity. Whatever you state here must be done as and when promised, otherwise you will look dishonest and/or incompetent. So make certain that you can carry out these actions before you set them down in writing.

5. Conclude with a brief apology for the unfortunate incident, but not for any errors on your part.

chasing a customer who has closed their account

Dear Ms Missen

Account: NW-908

Thank you for your letter of 28 September, closing your account with us.

I am extremely sorry to learn that you are unhappy with our services. We have made a careful note of your comments so that they can be passed on to the relevant departments and employees.

Your experiences with us are not typical of our customers and I would ask you to reconsider your decision and give us the opportunity to change your opinion of us for the better.

May we discuss this? Please call me on 01556 659834. This is my direct line.

I look forward to hearing from you.

With best wishes

Freddie Winters
Manager

---

comments

1. Those customers who write and make a point of closing their account (and complaining about products and/or services at the same time) are always worth pursuing, albeit diplomatically. Often they have taken their decision in anger or disappointment and may be persuaded to continue trading with your firm once they have calmed down, and their criticisms have been listened to and acted upon, as appropriate.

2. Acknowledge that the account has been closed as requested. Do not refuse to do this – however well intentioned such a refusal may be, it will only inflame the situation again.

3. Next, say how sorry you are to hear of their criticisms and indicate that they will be passed over to the relevant staff. You should be seen to accept and take the complaints seriously if you want the recipient to reopen their account. This is not the time to dispute the complaints or to defend yourself.

4. Stress that their view is not shared by your other customers and ask them to reconsider their decision. This gives you the chance to prove how good your products and services really are.
5. Encourage them to telephone you to discuss the matter. This allows you to explain your viewpoint and to win them over. If they do call, you know that your conciliatory letter has been a success!

handling purchases

When handling purchases, you are trying to obtain the best possible deal that you can from suppliers by writing letters asking for a discount, credit facilities, or extended or increased credit terms. Alternatively, you have to handle supply problems and difficulties, ranging from delayed deliveries to damaged and/or faulty goods. All need to be approached carefully.

enquiring about products and services

Dear Mr Hurst

I understand that your company supplies the Nurex range of window fittings and components, which we are interested in stocking.

With this in mind, I would be grateful if you would provide me with a sales brochure, price list and order form by return of post, along with details of your trading terms and conditions, and the current availability of these items.

Please note that at this stage we do not wish to be telephoned or visited by a sales representative, but will be in touch as soon as we have had an opportunity to study the various materials.

With good wishes

Your sincerely

Rod Fry
Manager

---

comments

1. The most difficult task with a letter like this is to ensure that you obtain the exact information you want in order to be able to decide whether you wish to take the matter further, but without leaving yourself open to those hard-sell telephone calls and visits that so often result from an enquiry of this nature.
2. In the first paragraph, simply express interest in the relevant goods and services. Be restrained, without sounding too keen or committed.
3. Next, say what you want, setting out everything you require and need to know about (to make your decision). Be very clear and precise.
4. In the last paragraph, state what you do not want – for example, telephone calls, and so on. Again, be specific. Conclude by saying what will happen next – you will be in touch with them, not vice versa.
5. Try to make this sound like a friendly, but matter-of-fact letter – you need to be firm but without giving offence.

accepting a quotation

Dear Mr Ravenscroft

Thank you for your quotation 824 of 14 March for the planned office extension alongside of our existing building at 76 Ranleigh Road, Dalton, Lancashire.

We are pleased to accept this quotation on the undestanding that:

- ■ The total cost will not exceed £7,500, as detailed in your quotation.
- ■ Payment will be made in three stages: £2,000 on signature of this agreement, £2,000 on 30 May and £3,500 on satisfactory and timely completion of the work.
- ■ Work will commence on 14 May and will be completed no later than 30 June, with the extension left ready for painting and decorating on that date.
- ■ You will work to the plans which were submitted to you by Holden Associates. Any queries concerning these should be directed to James Holden at Holden Associates, Mulberry House, York Road, Teignton, Lancashire TY23 9PT. Tel: 01010 444444.
- ■ Any other queries should be directed to me or, in my absence, to Julia Whitton at the above address. Our extension numbers are 223 and 547 respectively.

If these terms and conditions are agreeable to you, please sign and date the attached copy of this letter and return it to me at the above address. I will then arrange for a cheque for the initial instalment to be issued to you by our accounts department.

I look forward to working with you on this project.

With best wishes

Yours sincerely

Larry McLeish
Purchasing Manager

---

comments

1. When a quotation is accepted, it is essential that any key details not included in that quotation are agreed upon and set down in writing. Too often, such details are not agreed and this can lead to problems later on. If something goes wrong, for example, the buyer may insist that there was a verbal agreement, while the seller may be adamant that they were working to their normal terms of trade. Thus, a detailed letter, which is appropriate to the cost and complexity of the work and the risks involved, should be sent on acceptance of that quotation. (In complicated cases, it is wise to have a more formal agreement drafted by a solicitor.)

2. The main bullet-pointed part of the letter should focus on the issues of price, specifications, dates, terms and conditions, bonuses, penalties and any other matters that are appropriate to your individual circumstances, as relevant. After this, you need to ask for the recipient's agreement to these details. The easiest way of doing this is to enclose a copy of the letter and ask them to sign, date and return it to you.

rejecting a quotation

Dear Mr Meyer

Thank you very much indeed for your quotation of £11,500 plus VAT for the proposed office extension next to our existing property at 76 Ranleigh Road, Dalton, Lancashire.

We have studied this quotation carefully but regret to inform you that we are unable to accept it as the price is more than we would want to pay for this work.

Thank you again for giving us the opportunity to consider your quotation. We trust that we can approach you for other quotations on future occasions.

Yours sincerely

Larry McLeish
Purchasing Manager

comments

1. Too many prospective buyers of goods and services do not take the time or trouble to reject the quotations that they do not wish to pursue, typically because they feel awkward about the situation. It is worth sending a letter, though, to avoid embarrassing telephone calls or visits that might otherwise be made by would-be sellers, and to maintain good relations with them. After all, you may need to do business together at some stage in the future.

2. Write a brief, fairly standard letter, thanking the recipient for the quotation, indicating that you have studied

it carefully but cannot accept it for whatever reason, thanking them again and suggesting that you might contact them at some stage for further quotations. Such a letter should strike the difficult balance between being polite and friendly, but dismissive too – at least for the time being.

asking for a discount

Dear Ms Jamieson

Thank you for your 2000 sales catalogue and price list, which we have studied with great interest.

We would like to place an order of approximately £1,200 plus VAT with you, and are able to pay cash on collection. With this in mind, please confirm if you are willing to offer us a discount of 10 per cent of the total order.

We look forward to your response and to doing more business with you in due course.

Yours sincerely

Dana Haeri
Manager

comments

1. It is always worth asking for a discount, whether for a first-time transaction, payment in advance, on collection or delivery, or even for continued custom. Your letter should follow a set sequence.

2. Open by expressing interest in and enthusiasm for the goods and/or services. This implies that you are keen to buy, if the price is an agreeable one.

3. State what you plan to purchase, along with what you are looking for in terms of a discount. You may wish to ask for a little more than you would expect to be offered and are willing to accept if this is the type of company that seems to be willing to negotiate. Do suggest a figure rather than ask the recipient to say what is available, as their response may be seen as being the last word on the matter.

4. End by indicating that more business may be done together in the future, but be careful how you phrase this to avoid making it sound like a bribe or a threat.

requesting credit facilities

Dear Ms Riddleswick

We have recently obtained your 2000 sales and prices guide and are extremely interested in buying goods from your firm.

Therefore, we are writing to enquire whether we may open a credit account with you. We would be happy for you to approach the following for references about us:

■ Harold Mitchell, Corporate Manager, Midway Bank PLC, The Business Centre, Eveway, Staffordshire EV11 0PP.

■ Ben Lauper, Accounts Manager, Cripps & Sons Ltd, 9 High Road, Donnerton, Essex DO2 8YH. Tel: 01989 455372.

■ Trudi Wicks, Financial Controller, Right and Left, 44 Thretford Industrial Park, Thretford, Norfolk PP2 4DH. Tel: 01012 333434.

We await your reply and look forward to trading with you.

Yours sincerely

Molly Brandon
Manager

---

comments

1. Generally, it is advisable to request credit facilities as
    and when an account is to be opened, rather than later
    after you have been trading for some time on a pro
    forma, cash-on-collection or on-delivery basis. A
    request at a later stage may give a negative impression,
    suggesting that you cannot afford to pay as you have
    been doing, which may be regarded as a worrying sign.
2. Your letter should be written in a straightforward
    manner – ask for credit facilities, suggest a credit limit
    if you feel that this is appropriate, and provide bank
    and trade referees. Be wary of requesting a low credit
    limit, which may convey a defensive image, as if you
    cannot be trusted with a higher one. Try to supply two
    trade referees; ideally, these should be companies that
    are well known and respected in your trade or
    industry.

accepting a delayed delivery

Dear Mr Sealey

Thank you for your note of 8 September informing us that delivery of
our order 33 of 17 August will be delayed because of a shortage of
raw materials coming in from Italy.

I can confirm that we are prepared to accept this delay on the understanding that the goods will be delivered to us no later than 30 September. We do need them by then if we are to fulfil our own commitments to our customers.

If you cannot deliver by that date, please let us know upon receipt of this letter. We will make alternative arrangements on this occasion if we do not receive your confirmation by 17 September.

With good wishes

Yours sincerely

Meris Hoffman
Manager

---

comments

1. There is often a tough decision to be made whenever a supplier informs you that an order is going to be delayed, especially if they do not specify a rearranged delivery date for the goods. (Even if they do, it is still a good idea to send a letter of this kind.) Should you wait or go elsewhere? Your letter should strike a sensible balance between the two possibilities.

2. In the opening paragraph, acknowledge the fact that they have informed you of the delay and given you a reason. If they have not told you why, you may wish to ask. If you suspect that a larger firm's order has taken precedence over yours, this might influence your decision.

3. Indicate that you are prepared to wait, but only until a specified date (which should be early enough to allow you sufficient time to obtain replacements from

another source if necessary), and explain why you cannot accept delivery after that.

4. Finally, ask them to confirm whether they can deliver by then or not and say (politely) what you will do if they cannot – go elsewhere on this occasion. Do leave the way clear for any future transactions you may wish to make with them, though.

rejecting a delayed delivery

Dear Ms Laurie

Thank you for informing us that the PZ-200 models have still not been despatched by your European suppliers and are not expected to arrive in the UK until early next month.

Unfortunately, we do need to have these in stock by the end of this month at the latest in order to meet our own customers' orders.

Accordingly, we must cancel this order with you. We regret having to do this, but feel sure that you appreciate our position in the circumstances.

We look forward to placing further orders with you in the future.

Yours sincerely

Mary Duvall
Manager

comments

1. On occasions, you will not feel able to wait for delayed goods to be delivered, and will need to go elsewhere to

obtain the required items at the earliest opportunity. Usually, you will wish to cancel the order in a polite and friendly manner so that a good working relationship is maintained with the supplier.

2. Thank them for notifying you of the situation and explain as briefly as possible why you cannot wait, and keep this to the point, avoiding blame and accusations. Then cancel the order and indicate that you are looking forward to working with them again. Imply that this is just one of those things that happens in business from time to time.

complaining about damaged goods

Dear Miss Camplin

We received your delivery 247-97 of four packs of NK-550 units this morning and, upon opening them, discovered that 12 of the 16 units in one of the packs were broken and cannot be sold.

Please arrange for a replacement pack to be despatched at the earliest opportunity, to arrive here no later than 31 May. We would be grateful if you will collect the damaged pack at the same time as you deliver its replacement.

This is the third time this year that you have delivered damaged goods to us. This is not only inconvenient but causes us embarassment and potential financial losses if we are unable to fulfil our own obligations to customers. Please ensure that it does not happen again.

Yours sincerely

Ruth Greene
Manager

comments

1. Typically, this letter will need to be sent after you have received a delivery from a supplier and have signed a delivery note confirming that it arrived in a satisfactory condition. Having unpacked and discovered the damaged goods, you must write straight away to complain.

2. In the initial paragraph, set out the key facts: what was received and when, which items were damaged, and the consequences for you – unfulfilled orders, loss of sales, or whatever.

3. Specify what you want the recipient to do – usually, to collect the damaged goods and replace them at the earliest opportunity. You should set a deadline for receiving replacements, but make sure that it is realistic. It should be fairly soon to show that you mean business, but long enough for them to be able to do it by that time.

4. In the final paragraph, you may wish to develop your complaint, building on what you put in the opening one, as shown in this example. This would be particularly appropriate if it is an ongoing problem. Keep it factual rather than emotional, though – you should sound (understandably) aggrieved, but polite and in control.

5. Do not feel the need to draw attention to the fact that you signed the delivery note – after all, this is common practice if you are busy and do not have time to unpack each box and inspect every item. Referring to it will only distract from your (justified) complaint and make you sound defensive. But, in future, try to either open any packages or, if you do not have time, sign the receipt as 'goods received unopened'. This provides some legal protection.

complaining about faulty goods

Dear Mr Mulgrew

<u>Account 5493</u>

We purchased a Thomson Z-50 de luxe model from you on 30 March and have had continual problems with it since then. We have had to call out your service engineer on four occasions – on 17 and 29 April, 14 June and 29 July. These were for a variety of problems, as highlighted in the attached copies of the service reports.

As a consequence of the ongoing problems, we have now discovered that the framework of the unit has cracked along both sides, making it liable to break completely at any time and therefore dangerous to use. We enclose photographs and an engineer's report concerning this.

It is evident that we have purchased a faulty product from you and have suffered considerable inconvenience to date. We now face substantial financial losses. In the circumstances, we must ask you to replace this item with the same or a comparable model, and within the next seven days.

We await your prompt response.

Yours sincerely

Louise Carter
Manager

---

comments

1. It is always difficult to complain about faulty goods received from a supplier. If you write too gentle a

letter, you risk being rebuffed; if you are too fierce, relations may be damaged, perhaps irreparably. As with most letters of complaint, a fair but firm approach is most likely to produce the required response.

2. Begin by stating what you purchased and when, and expressing your dissatisfaction with the goods. Give the reason for this.

3. Provide some specific, fact-based background to the complaint, if appropriate. For example, if it is an ongoing problem, give dates and details of difficulties that have occurred. Support your comments with verifying evidence and from independent sources, whenever possible.

4. State what you want to be done to resolve your complaint and by when – perhaps a replacement or a refund, within the next seven days. Be polite, but very precise. Avoid threatening comments, but pursue the matter further if it has not been resolved satisfactorily by that time, stating that you will approach the trading standards officer at the local authority, take legal action, and so on, if necessary. Be prepared to carry through this threatened action, if you are to succeed.

complimenting a supplier

Dear Caroline

We purchased an IBX computer system from your firm earlier this year and are writing to say how pleased we are with it and the modifications that you made for us – they were exactly what we needed!

We are also very impressed with your after-sales service. We have called out your service consultant, John Tyler, for advice on three occasions, and he has always been most helpful and informative. Please pass on our compliments to him.

We are planning to expand our operation next year and will be in touch with you in due course to discuss our revised IT requirements.

Our compliments to you.

Yours

Lucie McLean
IT Co-ordinator

---

comments

1. Do take the time to write to firms to compliment them on their goods, services and/or employees, as and when it is well deserved. Too often, only letters of complaint are sent, but compliments can help to build and strengthen a relationship, which may prove useful later on during difficult trading times.
2. With this type of letter, the best advice that can be given is to keep your praise in proportion. If you praise a supplier too highly, it conveys the impression that you are writing for an ulterior motive, and can mark you out as smarmy and untrustworthy.
3. Compile a simple, straightforward letter, stating why you are writing, explaining briefly why you are pleased with the products, services and/or employees, and referring to continued custom in the future. The act of writing in this way is a compliment in itself.

criticising a supplier

Dear Mr Arnold

We write to express our dissatisfaction at the service provided by your firm under the terms of our service agreement. In particular:

- Our photocopier broke down on the morning of 17 September and you were notified of this immediately, although your service engineer did not call until the afternoon of 18 September, despite several reminders. This is contrary to the 'same day service' promise in the agreement. The delay caused problems for us.
- As the photocopier had to be returned to your workshop for repair, a loan model was supplied to us by your engineer, but unfortunately was not of the same standard. It did not produce colour copies, which are essential for our business.
- On its return, our photocopier was scratched and dented down one side. Although this does not affect its performance, this damage is unsightly and would not project a good image to those customers who see it in our reception area. We have now repositioned the photocopier so that the damage cannot be seen.

We feel sure that you will appreciate our unhappiness about these incidents, and trust you will take steps to ensure that they do not occur again.

We look forward to receiving your assurances on this matter.

Yours sincerely

Penny Risby
Manager

comments

1. Nowadays, people and organisations seem to complain about anything and everything, threatening legal action straight away and often for the most trivial of reasons. Inevitably, these actions create the strong impression that those complaining are petty and unreasonable. Not surprisingly, signs of aggression will damage (potential) working relationships, probably beyond repair.
2. It is far better to adopt a firm but reasonable approach. As with the preceding, complimentary letter on page 65, it is important that things are kept in proportion.
3. Start by stating that you are unhappy with the recipient's products, services and/or employees, as appropriate. Specify whatever it is you are dissatisfied with and how it has affected you. Use a bullet-point framework for easy reference, if it is relevant. Stick to the facts rather than opinions. Sound calm and reasonable. End by stating what you want to happen – a product to be replaced, services to be improved, an employee to be disciplined, or whatever.

asking for an increased credit limit

Dear Ms Patel

Account 2061

We write to apply for an increased credit limit on the above account from the current £2,500 to £5,000.

We are in the process of expanding our product range to meet increasing demand from our customers and will be making additional sales space available early next year to incorporate this expansion.

Given the diversity and quality of goods supplied by your company, we would prefer to purchase extra stocks from you rather than several other suppliers. Thus, we feel we need further credit facilities with you.

We trust that you are agreeable to this and look forward to receiving your confirmation at the earliest opportunity.

Yours sincerely

Liz Gibson
Purchasing Director

---

comments

1. This letter needs to be very positive. You're selling yourself here! Too many requests of this nature are made in a defensive manner. The writer addresses possible causes of rejection and provides counter-arguments in anticipation! As a consequence, doubts are put into the reader's mind.
2. In the initial paragraph, ask for an increased limit, referring to your account number, present and required limits. Get straight to the point to avoid confusion and misunderstandings.
3. State why you want an increase. This needs to be a positive comment, so make this an upbeat paragraph, full of positive words like 'growing' and 'expanding'.
4. Indicate that you would prefer to give your increased custom to them rather than to take it elsewhere. The suggestion that you might give your custom to a

competitor must be done extremely subtly, almost as if you are unaware of it. Make sure that it falls some way short of a hint and a long way away from a threat.

5. In the fourth paragraph, say that you trust, rather than (the more negative) 'hope', that improved credit facilities are acceptable, and that you look forward to receiving confirmation of this.

requesting extended credit facilities

Dear Mrs Hilter

Account EA-444

Owing to unexpected delays in receiving payments from our own customers, we are not yet in a position to settle the above account. We apologise to you for this situation.

We propose to settle this by four equal monthly payments of £750.25, commencing immediately. To this effect, I enclose a cheque for the first payment, along with three post-dated cheques to be presented at the appropriate times.

If the circumstances improve earlier than expected, we will notify you, of course, and settle the account straight away.

We trust that you are agreeable to this proposal and look forward to your response.

With good wishes

Yours sincerely

Anthea Wellman
Manager

comments

1. This is a far more difficult letter to compose than the preceding one asking for an increased credit limit, as shown on page 68. Even though both letters are written for the same basic reason – a need for more credit – the previous one can be viewed in a positive way, whereas the second cannot be seen in anything but a negative light. After all, the only believable reason why you want to delay or spread payments is because you cannot afford to pay at the agreed time, which is always a cause for concern to suppliers who may never treat you as generously again as a consequence of your action.

2. Write as soon as you know that there will be a problem. Begin by identifying it, giving a brief reason and apologising for the situation. Be careful not to make the reason sound like an excuse. Make an offer of settlement, enclosing an initial payment as a sign of good faith. It can be a good idea to submit post-dated cheques too, but only if you are sure that they will not be presented early (which might create cash-flow problems for you). Indicate that settlement will be made earlier if changing circumstances allow it. Finish by asking for their agreement to the proposal. If it is a reasonable one, this should be forthcoming and any damage to your reputation will be limited by the way you have handled the matter.

managing accounts

Accounts-related letters should be kept to a minimum, with invoices, statements, credit and debit notes being issued and payments received without extensive or difficult correspon-dence having to take place. Ideally, your letters should be limited to confirming balances, credit limits, payment dates and dealing with other straightforward matters. However, two types of letter that are especially difficult to write well are those that refuse credit and those that chase payments. Other letters that may cause concern are those that provide a reference about a customer, a response to a delayed payments proposal and an apology for an accounts error.

refusing credit facilities

Dear Mr Tracey

Thank you for your letter of 7 September, requesting credit facilities with us.

We have considered your request carefully, but regret to inform you that we cannot offer credit terms to you at this time. May we suggest that you re-apply when you have been trading with us for six months.

Meantime, may we thank you for your custom and inform you that paying on a pro forma basis entitles you to a substantial 5 per cent discount on all orders, including those for sale items. We enclose our latest sales catalogue for your perusal.

Assuring you of our best attention at all times.

Yours sincerely

Peter Hobson
Credit Controller

---

comments

1. More often than not, this type of letter has to be written at an early stage of your dealings with a new firm. It is difficult to compile, because, although they may well be reliable and credit worthy, they are an unknown quantity to you. Therefore, you are unwilling to offer credit to them until they have established a good track-record with you.
2. You need to make your rejection at the beginning of the letter, getting it out of the way as soon as possible. In the example, there is a very clear refusal at the start of the second paragraph – the recipient cannot be in any doubt about the exact position.
3. You can soften the refusal by being encouraging about the relationship and the future. In particular, this letter offers a review in six months' time. Even though the answer may still be 'no' – perhaps because the customer has a poor credit rating or history – the offer sounds fair and reasonable. Such a promise costs little, but means a lot.
4. Reminding the recipient of the benefits of the current

arrangement – discounts for prompt payment, or whatever – offers further encouragement to continue trading. The inclusion of a sales catalogue or something similar may even generate an order.

5. The whole letter has a positive and upbeat tone, which is essential if you want to continue doing business with this customer.

rejecting a request for an increased credit limit

Dear Sam

Account: 2034

Thank you for your letter of 5 March concerning the credit limit on your account.

We have considered this matter carefully, but are unable to adjust the credit limit at this time. As a small company, we have to operate within limited credit facilities.

However, we would be happy to give further consideration to this matter in six months. Please feel free to re-apply at this time.

Assuring you of our best attentions,

Yours

Ian Finlay
Accounts Manager

comments

1. This is a similar letter to the one refusing credit facilities shown on page 72, but is normally written to a more established customer who is seeking a higher credit limit than you are prepared to give. It is a more difficult letter to compile, though, because you may know each other better and you may feel obliged to give a reason for the rejection. If you do not, they will probably press you for it.
2. Acknowledge their request in your opening paragraph in order to focus their attention on the subject.
3. In the second paragraph, include the rejection and a fairly bland, all-purpose reason appropriate to your circumstances. This can be linked to the size of your firm, the need to maintain cash flow, or the current economic climate. The implication should be that you are rejecting increased credit limits in general, rather than this customer in particular.
4. Conclude with encouragement, suggesting that they re-apply at some point in the future. Even though the outcome then may be the same, you need to convey an open and receptive image to the customer.

requesting a reduction of an account balance

Dear Ms Ranibaldo

Account: 7898

We note from our records that you have exceeded the credit limit of £1,000 on your account. Your balance currently stands at £1,324.23.

To reduce your balance to within the agreed limit, please forward a cheque for the sum of £324.23 to us in the next 14 days.

We look forward to your response.

Your sincerely

Tony Dooley
Credit Controller

---

comments

1. If a customer exceeds their credit limit, it is the joint responsibility of the customer and the accounts department that allowed the situation to develop. Faced with such a scenario, you can either monitor it in the hope that the balance will be reduced in due course or, if you are concerned about the customer's ability to pay or their intentions, you can write to ask them to remedy the matter as soon as possible.
2. To avoid creating the potentially offensive impression that their account is causing alarm and being watched closely, it is wise at this stage to send what appears to be no more than a standardised reminder, which should refer to the agreed limit, the current balance and the sum required for payment and by when. If there is a possible problem with obtaining payment, other, stronger letters should be forwarded afterwards (see pages 77, 78 and 80).

chasing an overdue payment, first letter

Dear Mr Dawson

Account no 62435

We write to inform you that we do not appear to have received your payment of £595.75 for invoice 7809, dated 8 May. We would be grateful if you would give this matter your prompt attention.

If payment has been made in the past few days, please ignore this letter and accept our thanks for your payment.

Should you have any queries about your account, please do not hesitate to contact us on 01394 568439.

Yours sincerely

Angus Potter
Accounts Assistant

comments

1. At this point, you may suspect that you are dealing with a slow or reluctant payer but cannot be sure, so your letter must tread a careful line between getting paid as soon as possible and retaining their goodwill.
2. The first paragraph is a straightforward, fact-based reminder of the overdue bill. If there has been an oversight, you should be paid promptly.
3. In the second paragraph you can reduce the risk of causing offence if payment has just been made by acknowledging that this is a possibility and thanking

them for it. Always thank rather than apologise (as many letters of this nature do), because this conveys a positive instead of a negative impression.

4. In the final paragraph, you are inviting the recipient to contact you if they are having problems in making payment. If they do not pay up or call you immediately, you can be fairly sure that they are trying to delay or avoid paying you. So you will need to send a stronger reminder, as shown below.

chasing an overdue payment, second letter

Dear Mr Dawson

<u>Account no 62435</u>

Further to our letter of 22 July, we write to draw your attention again to the outstanding sum of £595.75 relating to invoice 7809, dated 8 May. This was due for payment by 8 June.

We wish to remind you that our terms of trade are strictly 30 days net. Please forward your payment within seven days of receipt of this letter.

Should you wish to discuss the matter, please contact us on 01394 568439.

We expect to receive payment no later than 15 August.

Yours sincerely

Doreen Platt
Accounts Supervisor

comments

1. Send this letter 7 or 14 days after the first reminder to show that you are monitoring the situation and are not going to let it drift. This impression can be reinforced if the letter is written and signed by someone higher up the organisation than the writer of the original letter – the accounts supervisor rather than an accounts assistant, for example – and by posting it by first class, recorded delivery.

2. Although the tone of the letter is much brisker, it remains polite. This is important – sarcasm and threats (tempting though they may be to include) could damage your reputation and standing in the business community. Also, if the matter does eventually go to court, you will need to show that you acted in a fair and reasonable manner at all times.

3. Be very firm, stating time limits for their response – 'within seven days', 'no later than 15 August'. Do not specify what will happen then or mention legal action, suspension of their account or whatever at this stage, though. You do not want to force a confrontation unless you have to, nor commit yourself to an unpleasant course of action that may still be avoidable. Remember, if you threaten something, you'll need to follow through on it (even if you don't really want to) or you will lose credibility. And if you've no credibility, you'll not get paid!

4. You must follow up this letter at the stated time if it is to have any effect – habitual bad payers will always take full advantage of slackness, indecision and good-natured suppliers.

chasing an overdue payment, third letter

Dear Mr Dawson

Account no 62435

We wrote to you on 22 July and 5 August, asking you to settle the outstanding sum of £595.75 relating to invoice 7809, dated 8 May. This sum is now more than two months overdue.

To date, we have not received any response from you and must now insist that this sum is paid in full no later than 22 August.

Failure to make payment by this date will result in your account being passed to our collections section to commence legal action to recover this debt, plus associated costs.

Yours sincerely

Sonia George
Credit Controller

---

comments

1. In many respects, this should be a similar letter to the second reminder – that is, brisk and matter-of-fact. You need to maintain a professional stance, taking care to avoid sounding angrier or increasingly desperate. A polite but persistent and determined approach will always be more effective.
2. The letter also needs to be handled in the same way. It should be signed by someone of greater authority than the last one, sent at a specified time (on the exact day

that payment was previously requested), and by first class, recorded post.

3. The key difference is that you should now state what will happen if the debt is not settled, and you must be prepared to carry out this threat and be seen to be doing it, if it is to have the desired effect of obtaining payment. If you cannot follow it through, the customer will realise that they can avoid paying you, and many will do so. It is important that you only threaten what you are prepared to carry out.

notifying a customer of legal action

Dear Mr Dawson

Account no 62435

You have ignored our letters of 22 July, 5 and 15 August asking for settlement of the outstanding sum of £595.75 for invoice 7809 of 8 May. This was due for payment by 8 June.

Your account has now been passed to the collections section, and I write to notify you that a County Court summons is being issued against you on 29 August for £595.75, plus costs.

If you wish to resolve this matter out of court, you must forward a cheque for £595.75 by 28 August.

No further notice will be issued to you.

Yours sincerely

Stephen Newby
Collections Manager

comments

1. At this late stage, it is evident that you are not going to be paid voluntarily and only imminent legal action, additional costs and a possible court judgment may have an effect.
2. In the initial paragraph, refer to the debt, when it was due to be paid and what you have done to try to secure payment from them. Keep this very matter-of-fact, avoiding any hint of emotion at all. (Bear in mind that you may wish to reproduce this letter for the court.)
3. State when the summons will be issued and how much it will be for. This should sound like a statement of fact rather than a threat. You need to appear calm and professional, rather than full of bluster.
4. Conclude by telling them what they must do if they want to stop this action, but indicate that no further correspondence will be issued. Be very specific about this, and then carry out the actions as and when stated. You have to – it's the only way you'll get your money.

notifying a customer of a suspended account

Dear Mrs Pellow

Account no 1298

Thank you for your order 76 of 18 January.

Unfortunately, we are unable to despatch this until your account has been brought up to date. At present, there is an outstanding balance of £623.98 due on 6 December.

We look forward to receiving your payment within the next seven days. Meantime, we are making up your order for you so that it is ready for immediate despatch on receipt of your cheque.

Yours

Bethan Thomas
Manager

---

comments

1. It is sensible to stop releasing goods to a customer if they have exceeded their credit limit and/or have fallen significantly behind on payments. However, it is unwise to write specifically to them about suspension unless you have to, as such a letter can cause ill feeling, with business consequently being taken elsewhere. Address the issue as and when necessary – for example, on receipt of an order.

2. In many ways, this letter is comparable to the first letter chasing an overdue payment on page 77. It contains a courteous reminder and conveys a positive image of everything being packed and prepared for delivery just as soon as the oversight has been remedied. In spite of the negative subject, this sounds a cheerful and upbeat letter.

3. The inclusion of the 'payment within seven days' line is of key significance as it puts a time limit on resolving the problem. If this customer is chancing their luck – trying to avoid paying and attempting to get more goods – their failure to respond will allow you to move on to send the second letter chasing an overdue payment, and so on. Seven days is the minimum time

period you should set. (Take postal delays into account.) Fourteen days is a fair alternative. Longer than that and this timescale loses its impact.

4. Always suspend rather than close an account while sums remain outstanding, as closure removes any incentive a customer may have for paying up and promptly. Only when the debt has been cleared should you consider closing the account, although even then it may be better to keep trading, albeit on a pro forma or cash-on-collection/delivery basis.

notifying a customer of withdrawn credit facilities

Dear Mr Preece

Thank you for your order 23 of 2 February.

Unfortunately, because of the recent difficulties with your account, we are not able to offer you credit facilities on this occasion.

If you would be so kind as to forward a cheque for £731.34, we will process your order straight away. Please note that this sum includes a 5 per cent prompt payment discount.

Assuring you of our best attention at all times,

Yours sincerely

Pat Baker
Sales Manager

comments

1. There will inevitably come a point with those customers who have a chequered payment history when you will no longer want to supply goods and services on credit – or at least not for the time being. Hence, a difficult letter will have to be written when you receive their next order – you want their custom, but without the financial risks involved with credit facilities.

2. After acknowledging the order, the first main paragraph should state that you cannot offer credit terms, and give a reason. Always include the phrase 'on this occasion' or something similar, to show that this is not necessarily a permanent situation, otherwise you will alienate them totally. Provide a broad reason: 'recent problems' or something comparable, is better than 'because we always have to threaten you with legal action to obtain payment from you'. Don't offend more than you have to (even if you want to!).

3. The second major paragraph should indicate the amount due and highlight the benefits of paying up front – for example, the order will be processed immediately and a prompt payment discount will be given. End on a positive note, assuring the recipient of your best attentions at all times.

providing a customer reference

Dear Mr Munglani

Thank you for your letter of 7 December, concerning Kaleidoscope of 174 Hamilton Road, Felstone, Suffolk IP2 0DF.

I can confirm that Kaleidoscope has been a regular customer of our firm for nine years. We have always valued its custom.

Please do not hesitate to contact me on 01234 987969 if I can be of further assistance to you.

Yours sincerely

Adam Doughty
Manager

---

comments

1. Providing a customer reference to a third party may seem straightforward enough – a good customer is given a glowing reference and a bad customer receives a poor one or even a blunt 'no comment' when you are approached. This can be inadvisable, though.
2. If a third party trades with a customer whom you have recommended and, for whatever reasons, they turn out to be less reliable in those dealings, this may then affect your relationship with the third party.
3. Should you provide a bad reference about a customer, and they find out about it, this will affect adversely your relations with them, or it might even lead to (threats of) legal action in extreme circumstances. Refusing to give a reference may have similar repercussions as well.
4. The most sensible way to approach a reference is to stick purely to the facts, avoiding praise, criticisms and opinions of any sort. Let the facts speak for themselves and allow the recipient to draw their own conclusions.
5. Avoid adding a disclaimer to the reference – for example, 'This information is given in good faith and

without recourse' or something similar. Not only is this unnecessary if you keep to the facts, but its inclusion suggests that you have no confidence in what you are saying or in the customer.

6. It is a good idea to offer to provide further assistance if the recipient wishes to telephone you. This will give you the chance to speak off the record, albeit still diplomatically, about the customer.

accepting a delayed payments proposal

Dear Jonquil

Account no 424
Outstanding balance: £2,872.80

Thank you for your letter of 12 March explaining your temporary financial circumstances.

We agree to your suggestion that you pay the outstanding balance of £2,872.80, as follows:

1 April	£718.20
1 May	£718.20
1 June	£718.20
1 July	£718.20

We suggest that you forward four post-dated cheques for these amounts and we will hold them until they are due to be presented. We look forward to receiving these by return of post.

Yours sincerely

Ron Morgan
Credit Controller

comments

1. If a customer has written asking for time to pay, this would imply that they are working through temporary difficulties in a responsible fashion. Assuming that their proposal is reasonable, it is usually sensible to respond in an agreeable manner. You will inevitably receive far less and over a longer period if you cannot come to an amicable compromise.

2. Be very specific about what you have agreed, listing payment amounts and dates, just in case problems arise later on. You should monitor these payments to ensure that they are received in full and on time, sending first, second and third chasing letters, and so on, if they fall behind (see pages 77, 78 and 80). You need to be fair, but strict, to secure all payments.

3. Alternatively, it may be a good idea to ask for payments to be made by post-dated cheques which you can retain for presentation at the appropriate times. If the recipient of the letter forwards these to you as requested, this would suggest that they intend to settle and will ensure that payments are not overlooked in a month or two. If they do not post the cheques, you can start chasing the outstanding debt straight away rather than in a month or so's time.

rejecting a delayed payments proposal

Dear Mr Mossman

Account: 7823
Balance: £3,642.96

We acknowledge receipt of your letter of 7 June and note your offer to settle the balance on your account by six monthly instalments of £607.16.

Unfortunately, we cannot agree to this proposal because of the length of time that this balance has been outstanding.

We are prepared to accept three monthly payments of £1,214.32, commencing by return of post. It is essential that this debt is cleared by the end of September to avoid further action being taken.

We expect to receive your first payment by 11 June.

Yours sincerely

Suzanne Aziz
Credit Control Officer

---

comments

1. Sometimes, an offer to repay an outstanding balance will not be acceptable, with lower payments being offered and over a longer period of time than you would want to agree to. Your response should follow a set sequence.
2. Acknowledge their offer in the first paragraph, but without commenting on it.
3. In the second paragraph, state that you cannot agree to it and give a reason – the balance has been due for some time, it is very large, you cannot provide extended credit facilities because you are a small, cash-conscious firm, or whatever.
4. To conclude, indicate what would be acceptable to you – assuming you are willing and able to offer a compromise – and make it clear that this is your one-and-only, take-it-or-leave-it offer. Always ask for the first payment by return of post to show that they are sincere.

5. If you are unwilling to spread payment of the debt, then your final paragraph should state this and specify a date by which full settlement must be made. If it is not received by that time, you can start issuing your chasing letters, as seen on pages 77, 78 and 80. (But do bear in mind that you cannot get money easily out of a failing business.)

apologising for an accounts error

Dear Ms Wells

Account 4241

Thank you for your letter of 12 December regarding your account.

I have investigated this matter and can confirm that credit note 132 was listed on your account as a debit note. We have not adjusted our records and enclose an amended statement for your perusal.

Please accept my apologies for this unfortunate incident. We are now introducing procedures to ensure that it does not occur again.

Should you have any further queries about your account, do not hesitate to contact me personally. My direct line is 0101 232 4545.

With good wishes

Yours sincerely

William Russell
Accounts Manager

comments

1. Accounting (and indeed, other) errors do happen now and then, and it is important that they are dealt with honestly and fairly if customer relations are to be maintained. To be effective, your letter has to acknowledge, explain, apologise, reassure and invite the recipient to contact you again if they have further queries.

2. Be careful not to give a detailed explanation of the cause of the error, as this is of little interest to the reader; they simply want you to admit to the mistake, to apologise for it and to tell them that it will not happen again.

3. Your apology should be sincere, but it can be kept relatively brief and simple, unless this is a serious mistake that has embarrassed or inconvenienced them significantly – perhaps they were unable to order essential supplies because of it. The more it has affected them, the more fulsome your apology must be. In extreme circumstances, you should offer some form of compensation – for example, you could waive payment of an outstanding bill.

4. Although you will hope that this will be the end of the matter, you must always give the recipient the opportunity to come back to you with further queries, otherwise your letter will sound dismissive, which you will want to avoid at all costs. Suggest that they contact you in person and offer your direct line or extension number, as relevant.

dealing with staff

Some of the most difficult letters you will have to write will be to employees who will be either joining the firm, working for it or leaving it. When recruiting, it is especially difficult to know how to reject job applicants and candidates, request references and make an offer of employment. You may wish to compliment or thank members of staff, or encourage them to do better – these letters must be handled carefully. To dismiss employees in a fair and reasonable manner, you must issue (verbal and then) written warnings before terminating their employment. Perhaps even more difficult, you may sometimes have to notify employees of impending redundancy, which is a painful task.

rejecting a job applicant

Dear Ms Fowler

Thank you for your application for the position of Data Processing Assistant.

We have considered your application carefully but regret to inform you that it has not been successful.

We would like to take this opportunity to thank you for your interest in Martland & Jones and to wish you well for the future.

Yours sincerely

Philip McCoy
Human Resources Director

---

comments

1. This is a tricky letter to write because you have conflicting aims. You want to be polite so that rejected applicants will continue to think highly of the firm, trade with it and apply for other (more suitable) vacancies in the future. At the same time, you do not wish to be too specific about the cause of rejection in case this leads to further time-wasting contact and possible disputes.
2. In the opening paragraph, you should simply acknowledge the application and refer to the appropriate job vacancy.
3. In the second paragraph, make a bland but firm rejection, expressing regret while making it clear that the decision is final. A brisk style can help to convey this impression.
4. Soften the rejection in the last paragraph by thanking them for their interest and wishing them well for the future.
5. In essence, this letter needs to be courteous, non-committal and dismissive, which is not an easy task! As a result, many businesses do not send letters of rejection at this stage, which is unwise because inevitably it causes greater disappointment and ill feeling than any letter could do.

inviting an applicant to a selection interview

Dear Mr Bullock

Thank you for your application for the post of Lecturer in Business Studies and Information Technology.

We would like to invite you to attend an interview for this vacancy at 11.30 am on Tuesday 3 November at our Bolton Street annexe. The interview will last for up to 45 minutes and will be conducted by David Smith, Head of Business Studies, and Amanda Jarvis, IT Co-ordinator.

A map of Otleigh is enclosed for your assistance. The Bolton Street annexe and the nearest car park are highlighted on it. Please report to reception on your arrival. Reasonable travelling expenses that have been incurred to attend the interview will be reimbursed at this stage.

We look forward to meeting you.

Yours sincerely

David Smith
Head of Business Studies

comments

1. It is common practice to telephone successful job applicants to invite them to an interview as this allows a mutually agreeable date, time and place to be set immediately. However, it is always sensible to follow

this with a letter confirming the main details. This should ensure that each candidate arrives as expected and without having to contact you again beforehand to check anything.

2. The main points include the date, time and place of the interview, its likely duration and brief details of the interviewer(s). You should put these at the start of the letter so they are absorbed quickly.

3. If the candidate has not been to the site before, always attach a map marking the location of the interview and other relevant places such as a railway station and car park on it. Without this information, some candidates will get lost and arrive late, throwing out your schedule. Refer to the map in the letter, otherwise it may be overlooked among any other material you are sending, such as sales literature. Also, instruct the candidate of the procedures to be followed upon their arrival. This can help to avoid embarrassment and confusion.

requesting a reference

Dear Mr Banks-Stewart

Ellen Winters has applied to us for the post of Office Assistant, details of which are attached. She has suggested that we approach you for reference purposes.

With this in mind, we would be grateful if you would answer the following questions. Your answers will be treated in the strictest confidence.

How long was Miss Winters employed by your company?
In what capacity was she employed?
How would you rate Miss Winters in relation to:

    a) ability;
    b) conduct;
    c) time-keeping;
    d) honesty;
    e) health?

Why did Miss Winters leave your employment?
Would you re-employ Miss Winters?

A stamped addressed envelope is enclosed for your reply. Alternatively, please do not hestitate to call me on 01898 898087 if you would prefer to discuss the matter.

Thanking you in anticipation.

Yours sincerely

Dee Hollins
Personnel Controller

---

comments

1. Typically, reference requests are sent out after you have interviewed someone for a job and are keen to employ them, subject to satisfactory references. This is an awkward letter to compose because you know that the referees are probably going to be firmly on the candidate's side, otherwise their details would not have been given to you!

2. You need to work hard to find out what the candidate is really like and whether or not they are right for you. Insisting on a reference from the candidate's current or most recent immediate superior may help you some

way towards achieving this. Don't be fobbed off with their own suggestions, who may be close friends and relatives!

3. To obtain a valid and informed response, always begin by providing brief details of the job so that the referee can assess if the candidate and the position are well matched. Attaching a job description is a good idea.

4. Ask direct and unavoidable questions about the candidate's length of employment, job and responsibilities, ability, conduct, time-keeping, honesty, health and any other issues relevant to this particular post. Asking why they left and whether the referee would re-employ them should produce revealing answers, too.

5. Encourage a prompt response by enclosing a first-class stamped addressed envelope and drawing the referee's attention to it in the concluding paragraph. Giving them the opportunity of telephoning you instead of writing is a sensible move. Few people will want to put criticisms in writing, and even those referees who are in favour of the candidate may reveal more than they intended when they chat informally to you on the telephone.

rejecting a job candidate

Dear Mr Cann

Thank you for attending an interview for the job of Warehouse Supervisor.

We have given your application careful consideration, but regret to say that you have not been successful on this occasion.

We are sorry if this is a disappointment, but hope you succeed in finding a suitable position soon.

Yours sincerely

Derek March
Personnel Manager

---

comments

1. In many respects, this is a very similar letter to the one sent to a rejected applicant, as shown on page 92. It has to be polite, vague but conclusive because you wish to retain the candidate's goodwill but do not want to encourage further contact, recriminations or arguments. The problem here, though, is that you have now met this person, may have established a rapport with them and feel that you need to explain and justify your decision. Resist it!

2. As before, write a brisk letter, acknowledging the candidates's attendance at an interview, making a bland rejection and wishing them well for the future. Do not go into details as this may lead to follow-up telephone calls and, in extreme situations, a claim being made against you to an industrial tribunal if the rejected candidate believes that they have suffered unfair discrimination during the selection process.

making an offer of employment

Dear Juan

Further to our recent meeting, I am pleased to offer you employment as a sales assistant based at our Great Wyeborough store. You will be responsible to the manager, George Roberts.

Your salary will be £12,200 per annum, paid by 12 monthly instalments into your bank account starting on the 20th day of the month following the commencement of your employment. The first payment will be made on a pro-rata basis. Overtime and overtime rates may be arranged by discussion with the store manager.

Your normal hours of work will be from 9.00 am to 5.30 pm, Mondays to Saturdays, with one day off during the week, by arrangement with the store manager. You will be entitled to a one-hour lunch break each day, by arrangement with the store manager. Your total hours of work per week will be 37½.

You will be entitled to 25 days' paid holiday each year, plus statutory holidays. Our holiday year runs from 1 April to 31 March. Your holiday entitlement from the commencement of employment to 31 March will be calculated on a pro-rata basis, and will be taken by arrangement with the store manager.

Other terms of employment that apply to all of our staff are detailed in the enclosed workers' handbook. Additional copies are available from the store manager on request.

Please confirm in writing if you wish to accept this offer and when you are able to start work so that we can make the necessary arrangements. Also, please give your written persmission for us to contact your present employers for reference purposes. This offer is subject to the receipt of satisfactory references.

I look forward to your response.

Yours sincerely

Carole Tompkins
Area Manager

comments

1. An offer of employment can be made orally or put in writing. It is sensible to make a written offer (or at least to follow an oral offer with written confirmation) as this will reduce the possibility of subsequent disagreements about the exact terms and conditions offered. With this type of letter, the contents are far more important than its style. Certain points need to be included (although their order can be varied to suit the circumstances).

2. In the first paragraph, make the offer and state the job title and location, plus the job title of the new employee's immediate superior.

3. Next, specify the salary – its amount, when and how it will be paid, overtime rates and arrangements, as appropriate.

4. Detail the hours of work per day, per week and in total. Mention lunch-breaks and days off as well.

5. Set out the holiday details – entitlements, when and how they should be arranged.

6. Refer to other terms and conditions of employment that are too lengthy or complex to explain in a letter, and state where information about them can be obtained – preferably in an accompanying handbook. (Do make sure that they have this information and understand it before they start work.)

7. In the concluding paragraph, ask them to confirm in writing whether they accept the offer, can specify a start date and you can contact their referees. As a precaution, make it clear that this offer is subject to the receipt of good references.

notifying changes in terms of employment

Dear Don

Following our discussion this morning, I am pleased to set out the changes in your terms and conditions of employment, as agreed at that meeting.

- ■ As from the week commencing 1 September, your day off will be on a Wednesday or by arrangement with your section leader.
- ■ As from 30 September, your salary will be paid direct to your bank account on the last working day of each month.

I enclose a copy of this letter for you to sign, date and return to me for our files.

With good wishes

Yours sincerely

Richard Goodfellow
Manager

comments

1. Like the preceding offer of employment on page 98, you must specify information about contractual changes in writing rather than relying on recollections of what was agreed verbally at a meeting. Too often, such recollections will differ as time passes and can be the cause of potentially significant disputes.

2. After a polite, explanatory introduction, set out the changes point by point down the page. This makes it easier for the recipient to read and absorb the information. Finish by asking them to sign, date and return a copy of the letter as confirmation of their agreement. This is very important and should be chased up at a later date if necessary.

complimenting an employee

Dear Gill

I just wanted to write to compliment you on the way in which you handled the Danbury contracts.

This was a very delicate and potentially disastrous situation. I thought that you dealt with it in an extremely courteous and professional manner. I was delighted with its successful outcome.

Well done – and keep up the good work!

All the best

Peter Vincent
Manager

comments

1. Most managers are aware of how much a verbal compliment can motivate an employee in the right circumstances, but a written one can have an even greater impact as it shows thought and effort, and often carries more weight and status because it is seen as formal, on-the-record praise.

2. To be effective, it needs to be kept very clear and simple – pay the compliment, give a concise explanation of why you think it is so deserved and congratulate the employee again. That is all you have to do – any further details will just weaken and even detract from the compliment.
3. Such a letter can be handwritten for an informal personal touch, or typed for a permanent, official record. Obviously, this choice rests with you, and your decision will depend upon your individual circumstances.

thanking an employee

Dear Chris

I am very grateful to you for managing the Smith & Porter project for me.

This was a detailed and complex matter and I know you had to spend a great deal of your time and energies on it.

I do appreciate what you have done and thank you again for your assistance.

With kind regards

Sarita Breadstill
Supervisor

comments

1. In many respects, this is a comparable letter to the last one, which complimented an employee on their work (see page 102). The main difference is that compliments can and should be made to employees, whereas thanks should be offered to colleagues of a similar status. Complimenting someone of a similar standing to yourself may seem patronising and could even offend them.
2. Keep your letter short and to the point – thank them, acknowledge how much they have helped you and thank them again. That is all you need to do to write a successful letter.
3. You can either type or write this letter by hand, depending on how well you know the recipient. A handwritten, thank-you note is usually more effective as it appears to have required greater thought and effort.

encouraging staff to do better

Dear Anna

As you know, we are always impressed by your hard work and the sales that you achieve for us. You are a valued employee.

However, sales have been low for some time now and we are looking at ways in which they can be improved in the near future.

With this in mind, we would like to work with you in order to identify why sales have dropped and what we can do to increase them.

Please consider this matter carefully over the next week or so and be ready to discuss it at our next sales meeting on 15 September.

We look forward to hearing your comments.

With good wishes

Peter Fitzwilliam
Sales Director

---

comments

1. This is a tough letter to write, especially if staff (believe that they) are doing their best. Phrased badly, this type of letter can demotivate employees quickly, and lead to ill feeling and disputes. 'Who the heck do they think they're talking to?' can be a common response to a letter of this nature, followed soon after by '...they know what they can do with it', or words to that effect. You must be at your most diplomatic when writing this letter.

2. You need to open by praising the employee, focusing on those attributes in which they take most pride – their hard work, for example. Such comments are reassuring and puts the rest of the letter into its proper context.

3. State that there is a problem and explain what it is: sales are falling, customers are complaining, production is behind schedule, goods are not being delivered on time, or whatever is appropriate in your circumstances. Add that you are looking at how this can be rectified and improved. Keep this paragraph factual, neither disguising your concern, nor exaggerating it.

4. You should close by indicating that you want to work together as a team to resolve this difficulty, asking them for their views and allowing them sufficient time to consider them before you propose a response, a tele-

phone conversation or a meeting in a week or two's time. Hopefully, they will then identify ways in which they can do better – albeit with your assistance.

first written warning about dismissal

Dear Miss Mitchell

I write to summarise our discussion of 11 May.

At present, I am dissatisfied with your attendance and time-keeping. In spite of previous verbal reminders on 20 April and 4 May, you have been late for work on two occasions this week, arriving at 9.20 on 8 May and at 9.30 on 10 May. On 11 May, you took an 80-minute lunch-break, returning to work at 2.20 pm. Your conduct is unacceptable and needs to change.

You have said that you will make every effort to improve over the next two weeks. We will help as much as possible by providing you with an advance on your wages so that you can repair your motorbike and will no longer be reliant on public transport. We will also put a clock in the staff rest-room so that you will know what the time is when you are in there.

It is essential that you reach and maintain the required standards of attendance and time-keeping, as specified in the enclosed operations handbook, by 25 May if the matter is not to be taken further.

We will meet again in my office at 11 am on 25 May to review the situation. If you have any problems prior to that, please do not hesitate to approach me at any time.

Yours sincerely

Davina Aitchinson
Office Supervisor

comments

1. A written warning should be given only if informal oral discussions and a formal oral warning have failed to improve an employee's performance, or if their conduct is sufficiently serious to warrant a written warning straight away. In either case, a written warning must not be issued lightly, as it is going to be put on the employee's file, and, if improvements are not made, may lead to dismissal in due course. Because of its potential consequences, this letter needs to be scrupulously fair, accurate and detailed – after all, if it is not, it could be used against you at an industrial tribunal in certain circumstances.

2. In the first paragraph, you should set out the reason(s) for the warning, supporting it with specific examples of the employee's misconduct. You should refer to previous verbal warnings if appropriate and how improvements have not been made or have not been good enough. Indicate that they must be made immediately.

3. With the next paragraph, you need to be seen to be fair – however unreasonable the employee may seem to be – in case the letter leads to dismissal and potentially to a tribunal. Say what you can and will do to help them to better their work rate and/or performance.

4. Finally, you should specify what standards have to be reached and by what date. State when you will review progress and stress that you are always available to provide further assistance, on request.

5. If sufficient improvements have been made by the time of this review, the employee can be congratulated and the written warning deleted from their file. Obviously, it is sensible to monitor them closely thereafter, though, to ensure that standards are maintained on an ongoing basis. Should insufficient improvements have been made, a second, and final, written warning may have to be given.

second written warning about dismissal

Dear Miss Mitchell

I write to specify the main points of our discussion of 25 May.

Despite two verbal warnings on 20 April and 4 May and a written warning on 11 May, your attendance and time-keeping remain unsatisfactory. You were late for work on 17, 21 and 23 May, and took more than the agreed length of time for lunch on 16 and 24 May.

I have agreed to give you until 1 June to improve and then to maintain your attendance and time-keeping to the required standards. Should you fail to do so, I will have no alternative but to terminate your employment.

We will meet again in my office at 11.30 am on 1 June.

Yours sincerely

Davina Aitchinson
Office Supervisor

---

comments

1. For continued unsatisfactory work performance or behaviour, a final written warning may have to be given to an employee. It is advisable to precede this with a meeting in which you can explain the reason(s) for your dissatisfaction. The employee will then be able to respond and tell you why improvements have not been made prior to this, as requested. You should be seen to be fair and reasonable at all times.
2. The meeting can be followed by a final written

warning specifying why you remain unhappy, what you want the employee to do and by what date, how this can be achieved and what will happen if it is not.

3. Essentially, this is the same basic letter as the first written warning. It needs to be fair, accurate and detailed, and to cover similar points. However, you must now make it absolutely clear that dismissal will follow and on a specified date, unless improvements are made by then, and sustained.

4. Keep a copy of this final warning on the employee's file. It can be removed if their performance and/or behaviour improves to acceptable levels. Otherwise, it will act as a record of the way in which you handled a difficult situation in a fair and responsible manner.

terminating employment, with notice

Dear Miss Mitchell

Further to our meeting of 1 June, we write to inform you that your employment with Hollis & Partners will terminate in two weeks' time on 15 June.

Your dismissal follows our verbal warnings of 20 April and 4 May, and our written warnings of 11 and 25 May. Unfortunately, we have seen no improvement in your attendance and time-keeping following these warnings.

We regret having to take this action, but your conduct has left us with no alternative.

Yours sincerely

Davina Aitchinson
Office Supervisor

comments

1. Dismissing a member of staff is a difficult and potentially hazardous task, leading to disputes and even attendance at a tribunal if it is not handled properly. For a dismissal to be fair, you must have sufficient reason to dismiss the employee *and* have acted reasonably at all times. To be sure of achieving this, dismissal must be seen as a last resort, being carried out only after several verbal and written warnings and chances to improve have been ignored.

2. In the first paragraph, you should notify the employee of their dismissal and give a termination date, in accordance with current legislation or their contract, as relevant.

3. Your reasons for dismissing them should be stated in the next paragraph, and references made to the verbal and written warnings given earlier. You should be seen to have been as fair and as reasonable as you could be.

4. In the last paragraph, you can indicate that you regret having to take this action but were left with no choice in the circumstances.

5. Often, it is wise to offer two weeks' wages (or whatever) in lieu of notice in order to remove a disgruntled employee from the premises at the earliest opportunity. If this is relevant to you, the final paragraph could deal with this issue: 'To resolve this matter promptly, I attach a cheque for £380 representing two weeks' wages in lieu of notice, and ask you to vacate the property as soon as possible after receiving this letter. Thank you.'

terminating employment, with immediate effect

Dear Ms Malcolm

Further to our conversation at 11 am, I write to dismiss you with immediate effect following your physical assault on Mrs Danvers.

Despite the seriousness of this assault, we have decided not to call in the police as we do not wish to prolong the matter any longer than is necessary.

A cheque for £398.56 is attached and represents two weeks' wages in lieu of notice.

Please vacate the premises forthwith. Your P45 and other documentation will be posted by first-class post to your home address at the end of the day.

Yours sincerely

Joshua Healey
Company Director

---

comments

1. On occasions, employees may need to be dismissed immediately after an act of gross misconduct. Although what constitutes 'gross misconduct' will vary from one business to another, such actions as a breach of confidentiality, theft, abusive or offensive behaviour or assault would normally be included within this definition by many firms. Even though the

employee may have already left the company, this letter should still be written, sent on and a copy kept on file to formalise the situation. It is important that you do not write it in an emotional state, which may lead you to be less circumspect in your comments than you would usually be. Adhering to a ready-made framework can help you to produce an appropriate letter.

2. The letter should be brief and simple. You should dismiss the employee and state the reason, indicate that you will not be taking the matter further as you want to conclude it as soon as possible, refer to the enclosed cheque in lieu of wages that would have been paid during the agreed notice period and ask them to leave the property straight away (if appropriate); any relevant documentation and other materials will follow on. Although it may be tempting to threaten them with legal action in some instances and to refuse to pay them any wages due, it is invariably more sensible to try to finish the matter with immediate effect to avert further unpleasantness.

terminating employment after a trial period

Dear Lee

Following your appraisal interview this morning, I write to confirm that we will not be making an offer of employment to you at the end of your trial period.

At our meetings of 17 September and 19 October, we identified a list of improvements that needed to be made to your work performance if you were to be offered permanent employment with us, and arranged a personal training schedule to assist you in making these improvements.

Unfortunately, these improvements have not been made and we do not feel that your work performance is of a sufficient standard to warrant an offer of employment.

Accordingly, you will leave us on Friday 29 November. Please call in to the administration office during that day to collect your final wages cheque and other documentation. Should you require a reference at any time, do not hesitate to suggest me as a refereee.

We wish you well for the future.

Yours sincerely

John Potts
Human Resources Controller

___

comments

1. This can be a difficult letter to write, especially if the recruit wishes to be offered employment, but is simply not up to doing the job properly. Ideally, the letter will not come as a complete surprise to them, though. You should have spoken informally about problems as and when these arose, and had meetings at which difficulties were raised and, hopefully, dealt with. You might even have issued one or two previous letters similar to the warnings on pages 106 and 108, albeit, perhaps, couched in more diplomatic language. None the less, dismissing a decent but incapable person is always unpleasant.
2. To begin with, state clearly that an offer of employment is not going to be made. You must be specific about this, leaving no room for any doubt, since this can lead to hopes being raised and unnecessary debate.

3. In the second paragraph, show how fair and reasonable you have been, in case they feel inclined to pursue a complaint of unfair discrimination against you at an industrial tribunal. Refer to what you have done to help them to reach and maintain the required standards of performance and conduct. Make this as brief and as factual as you can.

4. State that, despite this assistance, the required standards have not been achieved. It is sensible to keep this paragraph relatively short and even bland, as detailed specifics can cause distress and might be used as the basis of an argument or possibly a court case.

5. Be firm in the last paragraph, reminding the employee of the date that they will leave the company and what they should do on that day – for example, collect their wages, and so forth. Soften the blow a little by offering to provide a reference if requested, and wishing them well for the future.

notifying an employee of redundancy

Dear Petra

Further to our discussion on Monday, I regret to inform you that we have to make 25 per cent of our workforce redundant because of the need to rationalise our United Kingdom operation following the loss of our Scandanavian markets.

Based on our redundancy selection procedure for operatives of 'first in, last out', you will be made redundant on 30 September. We are very sorry.

In the two months up to 30 September, we will do everything possible to help you find alternative employment. Details of the assistance we can provide will be given to you by your section leader at your weekly team meeting on Friday.

You are eligible for a lump sum redundancy payment from us, based upon your age, length of employment with us and your current pay. This payment will be in excess of statutory requirements. Further details of this will be sent to you under separate cover by the end of the week.

Finally, I would like to say how saddened we are at having to take this action, unavoidable though it is. You have been a hard-working and conscientious employee, and we have enjoyed working with you over the past two years. We wish you every success in the future.

If you require any further information about the terms of your redundancy package or of the help available to you in finding new employment, do not hesitate to speak to me.

With sincere good wishes

Yours sincerely

Edwin Riches
Human Resources Executive

---

comments

1. Making a long-serving employee redundant is even more difficult than terminating someone's employment after a trial period of, perhaps, three months – inevitably, you will know them better and you may feel genuinely upset at having to notify them of what will be a dreadful blow. To produce an effective letter that is both factual and sympathetic, it is a good idea to work to a framework.
2. In the opening paragraph, tell them that they are being made redundant, why and when, and express et

3. State what you are going to do to help them to find alternative employment. You should be very realistic and avoid making promises, while you are in an emotional frame of mind, that you cannot keep later on.
4. Confirm whether they are eligible for a redundancy payment and give details, if appropriate.
5. Add some restrained personal comments – typically, expressing regret, complimenting them (after all, it is the job that is being made redundant not the person) and wishing them well for the future.
6. Conclude by inviting them to contact you for further information, or if they feel that you can offer them any other form of assistance.

providing a reference about an employee

Dear Ms Ginalska

Thank you for your letter of 6 October regarding Hayley Hubbard.

Hayley was employed by us as a machinist from 3 September 1993 to 31 October 1996. Her work rate and performance were of an acceptable standard at all times. She left to move closer to her family in Yorkshire.

Should you require further information, please do not hesitate to telephone me on 01384 697859.

Yours sincerely

Andrew Wright
Works Manager

comments

1. Giving a reference about an employee always seems easy – a good one is praised and a poor one is criticised. However, it is fraught with dangers. If someone is recruited because of your favourable reference and subsequently proves unacceptable, this may reflect badly on you. Likewise, if an employee is not taken on as a consequence of what you write, and they find out about it, they may come complaining to you, perhaps via their solicitor or an industrial tribunal.

2. The most sensible way to approach the situation is to stick purely and simply to the facts, which no one can dispute. Restrict your comments to the duration of their employment with your firm. Avoid offering your personal opinions. Always invite the recipient to telephone you if they wish to discuss the matter. This allows you to be a little more candid, although it is wise to remain guarded and to adhere as closely as possible to the facts.

attending to personal matters

Inevitably, you will have to write some tricky personal letters from time to time – for example, applying for jobs and responding to offers of employment, arranging and postponing meetings, and the like. On occasions, you will need to write about personal issues on behalf of your company, on matters as varied as congratulating an employee on the birth of their baby, to offering condolences on a death. These are all difficult letters to deal write.

applying for a job

Dear Miss Maslow

I write to apply for the post of project organiser, as advertised in today's *Evening Star*.

At the present time, I am working as a project co-ordinator at Berryman's, a publishing company in Blyfleet, Hertfordshire, that specialises in producing sales literature and promotional materials for local organisations. I am responsible for overseeing approximately eight projects each year, and co-ordinating all aspects of research and writing them, including the commissioning of freelance staff, as appropriate.

To do this job effectively requires self-initiative, the ability to schedule and prioritise tasks and to work to strict deadlines. As important, I need to work well with people – liaising with clients and organising researchers and writers in order to produce top-quality publications.

I am applying for the position of project organiser at your company because I am looking to progress from working on local accounts to those of a national and international nature. I have done all that I can do in Hertfordshire and am now seeking to develop my potential further. Your job offers me the opportunity to do this.

I have the skills, knowledge and expertise that you are looking for in the ideal employee. I have been working in a comparable job for five years and have won awards for it in 1997 and 1999. My Britpac project was commended in the Promo-1997 regional competition, which I won two years later with my Rococo project.

I also work in the same sector as Clinton-Rogers – in the past six months I have produced materials for Sebastian Bannister at Lewis & Williams, Edward Jones at Rochesters and Nikita Patel at Dawlish & Sons. Examples of these are enclosed for your perusal.

I would like to meet you to discuss this vacancy and my application for it in more detail. I am free every day next week, and would be happy to come to London to see you as and when you are available. My telephone number is 01324 354343.

I look forward to hearing from you.

Yours sincerely

Deborah Radford

comments

1. A job application letter should be sent only if you are asked to apply in this way. If you were told to submit a curriculum vitae, to telephone or to call in person, then a letter must not be forwarded, as you will be rejected straight away, not least because you cannot follow instructions! No one wants to employ a person who does not do as they are told. A letter of application should be no more than two pages long and fairly detailed.

2. Start by saying why you are writing, what job you are applying for and how you heard about it. This focuses the reader's attention, tells them what the letter is about and enables them to judge how effective they have been at advertising the post through various media.

3. Next, provide some concise information about yourself – ideally, those strengths that are most closely associated with this job, company and industry. These details may span perhaps two or three paragraphs.

4. State why you want the job. Use lively and upbeat expressions, with references to 'opportunities to progress', 'fulfil potential', and the like. Even if you are pursuing it for what might be considered to be negative reasons – for example, you are about to be made redundant, or whatever – you should still concentrate on making positive comments.

5. Explain what specific qualities you can bring to this particular position, linking your comments to what you know and/or can discover about the job and the type of person required by the organisation. You may be able to work from a job description and person specification supplied by the firm. Your qualities can be covered over two or three paragraphs.

6. The final paragraph should state what you want to happen next – for example, you would like to be telephoned for a discussion or invited for an interview. Encourage the reader to respond in the way that you want by providing them with your telephone number, a stamped addressed envelope for a reply, or whatever.

accepting a job offer

Dear Mr Laing

Thank you for your letter of 17 June, offering me the position of training instructor at Ridley's.

I am delighted to accept this offer subject to your confirmation that I am entitled to 25 days' paid holiday per year, plus statutory holidays, as discussed at our meeting of 11 June. This was not referred to in your offer of employment and I am keen to have this verified before I commence work.

I am happy for you to approach my current employer for reference purposes. My departmental manager is Sue Baxter and her direct line is 0191 349232. She is expecting your call.

I am able to start work on Monday 4 July, as suggested at our meeting, and I await your confirmation that this is agreeable to you.

I look forward to a long and successful career at Ridley's.

Yours sincerely

Judith Pearson

comments

1. You may be offered a job over the telephone or by
    letter. Assuming that you wish to accept the offer,
    it is sensible to put this acceptance in writing, not
    least because it gives you the chance to confirm or
    query the exact terms and conditions of that offer, as
    necessary.
2. If these terms and conditions have been dealt with only
    at an interview or via the telephone, then you can use
    this letter to specify them, perhaps in a similar way
    to the offer of employment letter shown on page 98.
    It is surprising how often verbal offers and assurances
    do not lead on to the job itself. It is more likely that
    they will do so if they are put in writing at an early
    stage.
3. If you have received a written offer of employment
    such as the one illustrated on page 98, your letter of
    acceptance gives you the opportunity to raise any
    queries about it, as shown in this example. You
    can also use the letter to grant permission for the
    prospective employer to approach your referees,
    if appropriate, and to suggest a starting date, as
    relevant.

rejecting a job offer

Dear Ms Puskas

Thank you for your letter of 26 November, offering me the position of
Data Processing Manager at your Oldbury division.

I have given this offer very careful consideration, but have decided
not to accept it. I do not feel it is the right move for me at this stage of
my career.

Thank you once again for your offer. I was very flattered to receive it.

Yours sincerely

Sally Rivers

---

comments

1. There may be occasions when you want to turn down the offer of a job; perhaps you were unimpressed by what you learned at a selection interview or have received a better offer from an alternative source. Whatever the circumstances, it is sensible to send a polite letter of rejection, just in case you wish to apply for another position there at some stage in the future.
2. Keep the letter short and simple. Acknowledge the offer. Say that you have considered it carefully, but have decided that it is not right for you at this time. Avoid specific comments or criticisms, as these might lead to further correspondence, and/or be held against you in any subsequent dealings. Thank them again for the offer and state how flattered you were to receive it.

asking for a meeting

Dear Dani

I am going to be in Yorkshire from 11 to 13 April inclusive, and would very much like to come and see you during that time to discuss your present stock arrangements.

We are about to launch an exciting new range of cameras and revised trading terms, both of which will be of great interest to you.

The new range is on a special introductory offer until the end of the month and applies to all orders taken in April. This will be my last visit to Yorkshire until July.

Why not give me a call now to arrange a meeting? My mobile number is 01212 212123, or call me at home in the evening on 01848 765901.

I look forward to your call.

All the best

Tracey Cooper

---

comments

1. Few people in business wish to be called upon unannounced, and it is not always wise to telephone them to request a meeting, especially if you are trying to sell something. Typically, you will be asked to describe your goods on the telephone, which is hard to do well enough to secure a meeting. Showing and demonstrating them on a face-to-face basis is usually better, and a well-written letter should help you to arrange a meeting to do this. The formula for success is straightforward.

2. Say what you want in the first paragraph – in this case, a meeting. There is nothing to be gained by being circumspect here, as this would only annoy or confuse the reader.

3. In the next paragraph, concentrate on telling them what is in it for them. It can be a good idea not to give too much away so that the recipient is keen to find out more and therefore to meet you. If you give away too much information too soon, they may make a decision immediately – and the answer may be 'no'.

4. To increase their desire to learn more, it is helpful if you can suggest in the following paragraph that some sort of offer is available, but only for a limited period. This might persuade them to act immediately.

5. Give them the chance to do so in the final paragraph by providing a contact number and encouraging them to ring it. Try to make sure you are available when they call so that a meeting can be arranged, at which you can make a sale.

rejecting a request to meet

Dear Mr Troughton

Thank you for your letter of 3 June, requesting a meeting to discuss our on-site catering facilities.

We are extremely happy with our existing arrangements and do not wish to consider any alternatives at the present time. Therefore, we do not feel that there is anything to be gained from a meeting in the foreseeable future.

Thank you for your interest in Damon Brown Exhibition Services.

Yours sincerely

Pat Booth
Organiser

comments

1. As a manager, you will probably receive an endless stream of letters from people who want to meet you,

usually to discuss the purchase of their products and/or services. It can be difficult to reject such requests, especially if you are not interested at present but might be in the future. Also, you may wish to remain on good terms with people offering you services, particularly if they are key players in your trade or industry. An encouraging, tactful rejection is required.

2. Acknowledge their approach and its reason, explain briefly that you are happy with the status quo 'for the time being' (or include a similar phrase), and thank them for their interest. Thus, you have turned them down in a polite and firm manner, but have still left them with an opportunity to contact you again at some stage, when circumstances may have altered.

postponing a meeting

Dear Ela

I am really sorry but I have to postpone our meeting scheduled for 2.30 pm on 9 December.

Unfortunately, I have to go to Middlewich on that day to attend a family funeral.

I will telephone you on my return on 11 December to arrange a meeting at the earliest opportunity. I am free most of the following week and hope that we can meet then.

With sincere apologies.

Kind regards

Les McDonald

comments

1. On occasions, you will have to postpone a meeting, perhaps for personal reasons such as an illness or a death in the family. By postponing, you run the risk of offending the recipient who may believe that this is an excuse because you do not really want to meet; it could even lead to the cancellation of the meeting and the loss of any consequent business unless the postponement is handled carefully.

2. Write as soon as you know that you will have to postpone. Apologise for postponing – do so profusely, the closer it is to the meeting. Give the reason – and this must be a justifiable one – if you are to avoid causing offence. Pressure of work, for example, is not serious enough. Inevitably, the other person will feel they are just as busy as you, if not more so! End by stating exactly when you will contact them to rearrange your meeting, indicating when you will be free to meet, so they know that you are sincere. Then get in touch, as promised.

introducing an associate

Dear Nic

I write to introduce Neville Boswell to you. Neville worked as a sales representative for me at Illeys from 1994 to 1999, when he left to set up his own sales agency.

I understand that he is currently acting for Drapers, Samways, Decker & Hudson, and Rampton & Sons, and is seeking to expand his territory into the West Country. He has asked me to introduce him to selected firms in this area before he contacts you to arrange a meeting.

I am sure you would be interested to see him and what he has to offer.

Yours sincerely

Paul Fox
Sales Director

---

comments

1. In the course of your work, you will occasionally be asked by an associate to introduce them to a third party – typically, someone they can do business with. Hopefully, this request will come from a person whom you know well, respect and are happy to recommend, although you should still be careful. If they do not live up to your recommendations, it could damage your reputation and your relationship with the third party. Therefore, try to give facts rather than opinions in your letter of introduction, and let the recipient come to their own conclusions.
2. In the first paragraph, say why you are writing, how (well) you know the person you are introducing and what they do.
3. Next, provide further details about your associate – more about what they do, why they wanted you to contact the recipient, and the like. Keep this very brief and factual.
4. In the last paragraph, make a pleasant but relatively bland comment suggesting that it may be worthwhile for them to meet or to speak on the telephone, as appropriate.
5. Be wary of making any firm recommendations, unless

you are totally confident in the associate's ability to match them and are happy to have your reputation linked closely with theirs in the mind of the recipient of this letter. Always keep to the undisputed facts, rather than disputed opinions.

thanking someone for an introduction

Dear Paul

Thank you very much for introducing me to your business contacts in the West Country. I visited them last week, taking several orders and establishing what I hope will prove to be long-term relationships with them.

I have no doubt that your introductions made all the difference to the welcome I received from them, and I am extremely grateful to you for this. Thank you again.

If I can ever do a favour in return, please do not hesitate to contact me.

With very best wishes

Sincerely

Nic Boswell

comments

1. You should always acknowledge someone's help in business, whether they have introduced you to a third party, provided a reference, or whatever. A short,

handwritten note is a nice touch, and makes it more likely that they will help you again on future occasions. Get into the habit of sending thank-you letters, if you do not already do so.

2. Keep it simple: thank them for what they have done, explain briefly how it helped you (and made all the difference), and offer to return the favour as and when requested. You can conclude by thanking them again.

congratulating someone on an award

Dear Nigel

I just wanted to drop you a line to congratulate you on winning the Harvey–Prescott award last week.

It really is a terrific achievement and well deserved. You must be feeling very happy.

Once again, congratulations to you.

Kind regards

Gilbert O'Reilly

comments

1. If a colleague at work or an associate at another company has won an award, you may feel obliged to write a letter of congratulations to them. This requires some thought and attention, though. You need to avoid sounding unctuous if they are in a position to help you in some way. At the other extreme, you have

to be careful not to appear bitter if you were an unsuccessful rival for that award, nor do you want to overcompensate by being too cheery.

2. Congratulate them, praise the award, say how much they deserve it and congratulate them again in conclusion – that is all you need to do to write an effective letter.

3. Convey a friendly and informal impression by using relaxed expressions such as 'drop you a line' and 'kind regards'. Build on this by writing by hand and in a card, if you can find a suitable one – perhaps something that reflects in some way the award that was given.

thanking someone for an award

Dear Georgina

I am absolutely delighted to learn that I am to receive the Innovate 2000 award at next month's trade show at Harrowfield.

I have always worked towards developing new and innovative products and to be given this award means that this is recognised throughout the industry.

It really is a terrific honour both for me and D-Brief, which has always supported and encouraged my endeavours.

Thank you.

Yours sincerely

Dennis Ramsden
Designer

comments

1. If you have been honoured with an award of any kind, it is sensible to write an enthusiastic but essentially modest letter of thanks to the organisers. This will create the best possible impression of you and your firm.
2. In the opening paragraph, express delight and perhaps surprise that you have been selected for this honour.
3. State why you think you were chosen, taking care not to sound arrogant and big-headed.
4. In the closing paragraph, say that this is 'a tremendous honour' (or something similar), and pay tribute to those people and/or organisations that have helped you to achieve it.
5. Sending a handwritten letter on letterheaded notepaper is probably the most appropriate way of conveying a formal recognition of an award with a highly personal touch.

thanking someone for a present

Dear Gerry

I just wanted to write to thank everyone for the lovely ornament that you gave me. It was such a surprise!

This is an unusual and imaginative gift, and I will think of you all with happy memories whenever I look at it.

Once again, thank you. I appreciate your kindness.

Good wishes to everyone

Tara Horton

comments

1. This can be an easy letter to write if you like the gift, but is much more difficult to compose if you do not – unless you pretend that you do!
2. Start by thanking the person for what you have been given – naming it sounds warmer and more friendly than writing 'the gift' or 'the present'. Add an excited comment – 'fantastic', 'marvellous', 'a surprise' – followed by an exclamation mark. This will have a positive, upbeat effect on the recipient. Then say something complimentary about the gift – that it is what you wanted and/or will remind you of them. Conclude by thanking them again and wishing them well.
3. For such a personal matter, this should be a hand-written and informal note, on A5 notepaper, and without all the usual, formal entries. You should set it out in the way that you feel reflects your individual style. It would be equally appropriate in a small card or thank-you notelet.

congratulating someone on the birth of their baby

Dear Naomi

All of us here in the office are delighted to hear that you have had a baby boy and want to send our very best wishes to you, Nick and the new arrival!

We enclose a small present with our warmest regards. Do let us know how you are getting along once you have settled back at home.

All the best

Everyone!

comments

1. It can often be difficult to know whether or not to write to a business colleague or associate who has just given birth – you probably do not wish to seem too forward, especially if you do not know the person very well, nor do you want to appear rude by apparently ignoring such a momentous occasion in their life. A brief, carefully composed note may be a sensible compromise.

2. Say how delighted you are to hear the news, and send your best wishes. Write on behalf of 'everyone' to convey universal excitement and interest. If you are uncertain of the baby's sex, name or its spelling, refer to 'your baby', 'baby girl' or even 'your new arrival', as relevant – don't risk causing offence by getting the details wrong. Include their partner in this greeting, if they have one. Put 'your partner', if you are unsure of the exact details of their relationship.

3. Draw attention to any small gift you may have enclosed with the letter. It is difficult to know what to give but, hopefully, someone who knows the recipient can advise you accordingly. If in doubt, a small teddy bear or perhaps white or lemon-coloured sleep-suits are fairly sensible choices. Invite them to contact you with the latest news when they are ready to; never indicate that you intend or would like to come to see them, unless you know them extremely well and are sure that this would be welcomed.

4. As with the previous thank-you letter, this should be a personalised, handwritten note, either on A5 paper or in a congratulations card. Do not worry too much about the exact dos and don'ts of letter-writing – conveying enthusiasm and excitement is far more important here.

congratulating someone on their promotion

Dear Ian

I have just heard that you have been chosen to head the Customer Relations Department at the new Swanleigh division and wanted to write to congratulate you on this well-deserved promotion.

I realise that you must be extremely busy at the moment, but hope we will have the opportunity to have a chat before your move.

Wishing you well

Yours sincerely

Elmer Williams
District Co-ordinator

comments

1. This type of letter can serve an important purpose, conveying a positive impression of you (and your firm) on someone in authority with whom you can do business. However, it is a tricky one to write, as potentially it can sound patronising, bitter or even ingratiating, depending on whether the recipient is below, alongside of or above you in the organisation. If the move is more of a sideways transfer than an upwards promotion, such a letter may not even be welcome at all.

2. Generally, the best way of approaching this is simply to acknowledge the move, congratulate them on it and wish them well for the future. Write a plain, straightforward letter that cannot be misinterpreted or viewed in any way other than a statement of congratulations. If you suspect that this is more of a transfer than a

promotion, you might wish to add a middle paragraph, referring to the challenges and opportunities
that lie ahead, which implies that you believe that this
is a worthy and fulfilling move. Get them to look on
the bright side!

congratulating someone on their retirement

Dear Cyril

Following your retirement dinner, I couldn't help remembering how long you'd been wish us here at Kingston's – it's been over 25 years, hasn't it?

I then felt I just had to write to thank you personally for everything you've done for us in that time, especially in Despatch. There were times when it was hard to imagine we'd have had anything delivered on time without you organising everything so smoothly for us.

I'm sure I'll never forget your sense of humour under pressure, and particularly that day last summer when we had 32 loads come in together – you got them out on time, too. I couldn't believe you did it!

You will be missed by everyone here at the firm, and we all wish you and Edna every happiness in the future.

I'm sure you'll be spending lots of time on your bird-watching from now on, but do drop in to see us from time to time. We'll be pleased to see you.

Kindest regards

Ron Davies
Managing Director

comments

1. Any employee who is retiring deserves a letter of recognition, especially if they have worked for the organisation for some time. It should be written by someone of significance in the company, not their immediate superior.

2. The first paragraph should reflect on the length of time that they have been with the firm and be couched in terms of admiration.

3. Pay tribute to their role in and significance to the organisation in the next paragraph, focusing on a skill or quality that they are particularly proud of and acknowledging it.

4. In the third paragraph, recall a memorable incident that highlighted their abilities and shows them in a favourable light.

5. Draw towards a conclusion by telling them how much they will be missed by everyone and wishing them (and their partner, if appropriate) well for the future.

6. End by suggesting that they stay in touch and call in occasionally because you would be pleased to see them.

7. Do make this a very personal, touching letter – retirement is a momentous occasion in everyone's life and should be handled as such. Use first names and write by hand to show how special it is.

8. Ensure that the letter is very positive and upbeat too – after all, this is a transitional period that is viewed with mixed feelings by many people. Try to refer to the good points of retirement – the chance to spend more time with a partner, visit family and pursue hobbies.

sympathising about a business failure

Dear Jonathan

I am really sorry to learn that AMZ is to close down on 30 September after trading in Colnebury for 25 years.

I was aware of the problems you had been having with your European markets and had hoped that you would overcome them, but now realise that they were much worse than I had imagined.

It has been a pleasure to work with you over the years, and I hope that you and everyone else in the company are successful in finding alternative employment in the near future.

My best wishes to you

Kind regards

David Preston
Manager

---

comments

1. You may be on friendly terms with owners, managers or employees at a firm that is to cease trading, and might wish to write to one or more of them to express your sympathies. This can also be a wise business move, as they could then recommend that their customers approach you for goods and services on future occasions.

2. Keep the letter short and simple – express sympathy about the forthcoming closure, refer to the reasons for it in broad terms, compliment the recipient and the

other employees and wish them well for the future. Do not labour the points – the actual act of writing should in itself fulfil your aims of offering sympathy and encouraging them to redirect their trade to your concern.

3. Given the nature of this correspondence, it may be appropriate to send a handwritten rather than a typed letter

sympathising about illness

Dear Edward

Everyone here in Personnel is sorry to learn that you aren't feeling well at the moment and wanted to let you know that we are thinking of you.

Don't worry about your work at all – Jack and Laura are handling it between them until you're better.

Take good care of yourself. We look forward to seeing you in the office only when you are back on your feet again.

With our best wishes

Tom and all in Personnel

comments

1. When someone is ill and off sick for an extended period, you may feel obliged to write to extend your sympathy and best wishes to them, but could feel uncertain about what to write, especially if the illness

is serious or even life-threatening. A positive but non-demanding letter is often the most appropriate. Adhering to a basic framework, adapted to suit your own circumstances, can be a good idea.

2. In the opening paragraph, express sympathy. Refer to 'we' or something similar if possible, to indicate that everyone is concerned and feels the same.

3. Many people who have been taken ill are worried that their colleagues cannot handle their work for them and that it will be piled up on their return. Deal with this in a brief but reassuring manner in the next paragraph. Others may be concerned that they'll be replaced in their absence, so do make a point of referring to them coming back, or similar. 'Until you're better' is used in the example.

4. In the last paragraph, extend your best wishes and indicate that the recipient should come back to work only when they are ready to do so. Even if you believe that they are unlikely to return, it is wise to make remarks of this kind to sound positive and uplifting.

5. It is probably most appropriate to write this type of correspondence by hand, and in a card rather than a letter. Choose a card with a nondescript front – a view, for example – rather than one that refers to illness, which can be depressing and downbeat to receive.

sympathising about hospitalisation

Dear Emma

We were all sorry to hear that you are in hospital and send you our best wishes.

Deborah has promised to let us know how you are getting along. Do tell her if there is anything we can do for you during your stay – we would be only too pleased to help in whatever way we can.

Meantime, don't worry about your work – we are looking after everything while you are away. Come back only when you are good and ready.

Kindest regards

Joan Mitchum

---

comments

1. In many ways, this is a comparable letter to the one sent to someone who is ill (see page 139). The same basic points apply, and the framework should be similar too – we are sorry, your work is being taken care of, don't return until you feel able to do so, and so on.

2. The main difference is that it is particularly tricky to know whether to visit someone who is in hospital. You may upset them if you do and they do not want visitors; you might offend them if you don't and they would like to be visited. It is a 'no-win' situation. Probably the best approach is to indicate that you are keeping in touch with their partner, a close friend or someone who knows them well so that the recipient can advise them, as relevant. Saying that you would be happy to help in whatever way you can, if asked, is a nice touch as well.

sympathising about redundancy

Dear Keith

I was surprised and disappointed to hear that Tatchells is making you redundant next month. Sadly, this does seem to be a common occurrence at the present time.

Of course, you still have so much to offer to an employer in the trade – an unrivalled knowledge built up over 20 years, terrific selling skills, and experience across all sectors of the industry. These attributes will always be in demand and I am sure that you will be back at work very soon.

If there is anything I can do to help you, please do not hesitate to call me. My direct line is 01112 323232.

Yours

Ned Lavender

comments

1. You may want to write to someone who is being made redundant for personal reasons – typically, they have been good to you in the past and you are sorry to learn of the news. It can be advantageous in business terms, too, though – they might be re-employed in a comparable or better position soon and will remember your kind gesture at that time.

2. In the first paragraph, express surprise and regret at the news of their redundancy. Indicating that it is not unusual these days may re-assure someone who has taken the redundancy as a personal affront – it is the job rather than the person that is being made redun-

dant, and it is no reflection on them, or something similar.

3. An encouraging and uplifting second paragraph is needed, reminding them of what they have to offer. Mention those skills and areas of expertise that they have that are most readily transferable to other positions. Say how important these are and how they are always in demand.

4. If you are indebted to this person – perhaps they have introduced you to prospective customers in the past, for example – then you might wish to end by inviting them to contact you if you can be of any help. Even if you can only offer limited practical assistance, they may welcome the opportunity to talk things over with a sympathetic colleague in the trade.

offering condolences on a death

Elsie

I write on behalf of everyone at Pollards to tell you how very distressed we are to learn of Mick's death.

Mick was an accomplished and hugely popular sales representative. He will be missed by everyone here, his clients in Wales and his many friends in the industry.

We send our sincere condolences to you. If there is anything we can do for you now or in the future, please let us know. We would be only too pleased to help.

Sincerely

Alec

comments

1. For many people, writing to someone whose partner, close relative or friend has died is a difficult task. Typically, they want to say enough to show how sorry they are, but not so much that it distresses the recipient even further. Often, adhering to a basic framework can be helpful.

2. Start by saying how sorry everyone is to hear of the person's death. Do not mention the cause of death as this is unnecessary and may be upsetting if it was sudden. Avoid euphemisms like 'gone to sleep', which make you sound awkward and embarrassed.

3. Pay a simple but sincere tribute to whoever has died, focusing mainly on their personal qualities, how popular they were and how much they will be missed rather than their business skills and success. After all, the recipient of your letter is the person's husband, wife or partner, not a business colleague.

4. End by offering your condolences and stating that you are there to help, if asked. This can be stressed to show it is a genuine offer, but that you do not want to push yourself forward, unless invited.

5. Do write by hand, removing as many of the formalities as you can in order to personalise the letter as much as possible.

6. You may like to write in a card rather than sending a straightforward letter. Pick one that seems to suit the recipient – some cards, for example, are very sentimental, which many people find false and insincere. Select one with a blank interior so that you can write your note in your own words rather than relying on a copywriter's sentiments.

writing miscellaneous letters

All sorts of letters may have to be written by you as part of your job, many of which are sent infrequently. This can sometimes make them more difficult to write because you simply have not had enough practice at composing them. Some of the more difficult ones include thanking someone for a donation, complaining about media coverage and, sadly, announcing a death.

requesting a donation

Dear Mrs Singleton

Candler & Sons has set up a fund for Alistair Martin, the six-year-old son of Helen Martin, one of our packers. Alistair has been diagnosed with leukaemia and we are hoping to raise £3,000 by the beginning of the summer holidays so that we can send him and his family to Funworld in America.

Any money that is raised over that amount will be donated to the C–Kers organisation. This is a local charity that has worked with sick children in Fenleigh for more than ten years. A leaflet about C–Kers and their activities is enclosed for your perusal.

We hope that you will contribute something to this fund. Cheques should be made payable to 'The Alistair Martin Fund' and forwarded to Caroline Reid at the above address. Alternatively, cheques or cash can be paid direct to the fund at the Midchester Bank, 18 High Street, Midchester, Sussex BN17 4LL. The sort code is 20–98–07 and the account number is 70603090.

For further information, please do not hesitate to telephone Caroline or me on 01212 232436, extensions 34 and 79 respectively.

We look forward to your response.

Many thanks indeed

Madeleine Platek
Chief Administrator

---

comments

1. Requesting a donation is a difficult letter to write. You may be emotionally involved with the cause, which means that you are more likely to compose a heart-felt and emotive letter, perhaps missing out some of the key facts as a consequence. Alternatively, there is a temptation to produce something like a sales letter, trying to manipulate the reader through emotional blackmail. If the cause is a worthy one, it is often best to let the facts speak for themselves, as in the example.
2. The key information – who has set up the fund, for

whom and why, and what the targets are – should be stated in the initial paragraph, to put the message across straight away. Do not overplay the good or serious nature of the cause as this will make it sound like a begging or hard-sell letter – if the subject is close to the reader's heart, the basic facts should be sufficient.

3. The second paragraph of the example explains where any excess donations will go once the target figure has been reached. This is worth covering if you are in a comparable situation, because this thought will have occurred to prospective givers, who may be reluctant to donate anything without this information, especially to a non-recognised cause. You have to be careful here, though – if people are not interested in or disapprove of the charity, they may not give at all. Make sure that it is closely associated with the main cause.

4. The next paragraph should tell the recipient how they can make a contribution – to whom cheques should be made out, and where they should be sent or paid in. Many people will be suspicious of, and therefore reluctant to donate to, anything that seems remotely amateurish and potentially fraudulent. Thus, it is essential that donations are made to a named fund with a separate bank account.

5. Always conclude by giving the reader the opportunity to find out more by providing them with a contact name and telephone number. Waverers may be persuaded to pick up the telephone and call for additional information, thus giving you an opportunity to secure a donation from them.

thanking someone for a donation

Dear Mrs Singleton

Thank you very much indeed for your contribution of £25 towards The Alistair Martin Fund.

With the assistance of generous firms and people such as yourself, we have so far collected £1,279 towards our target of £3,000 to send Alistair and his family to Funworld in America.

Many thanks again for your kind donation.

Best regards

Madeleine Platek
Chief Administrator

comments

1. This type of simple and straightforward thank-you letter is sent rarely, if at all, to those people who have made modest donations. It is argued that the money spent on such correspondence is better directed to the good cause. However, thanking someone for a donation is courteous, increases their goodwill towards the cause, and makes it more likely that they will contribute to it again in the future. If the target figure has not been achieved to date, they might even make a further donation in response to this letter.

2. In the first paragraph, acknowledge the donation made to the cause. The second paragraph should contain an update on how the fund is building up to the target figure. If it is nearly there but not quite, this is most likely to generate additional donations from previous givers. End by thanking them again for their donation.

refusing a charitable request

Dear Mr Greening

Thank you for your letter of 11 August, asking for a donation to your Penny-Wise Fund.

We receive many letters of this nature and, unfortunately, it is not possible for us to respond favourably to all of them. We have a limited budget for charitable donations and it is fully committed at this time.

Therefore, we are unable to make a contribution on this occasion. We wish you well in your approaches to other organisations.

With good wishes

Yours sincerely

Jeremy Clarke
Public Relations Officer

comments

1. A letter of this kind needs to be handled carefully. Whatever your reasons for rejection, you will not wish to be seen as being heartless in case this has an adverse effect on your reputation within the community. At the same time, you need to be firm so that the recipient does not try to pursue the matter any further.

2. With this in mind, you should thank them for their letter, suggest that you are always inundated with requests like this, would like to give freely but cannot afford to do so, and then decline the request politely, wishing them well. Keep it as short and as simple as that.

asking a favour

Dear Jed

I write to ask if you can do a favour for me.

We are planning a conference on better business communications for later in the year and are looking for speakers. I recall that you had an excellent speaker on video-conferencing at your 1999 Comm-Ex exhibition – a Canadian woman who had just been transferred to the United Kingdom by her company, I believe.

Do you have a contact address or telephone number that you can let me have, so that we can approach her? I would really appreciate your help. Perhaps you will call me on my direct line: 01235 324324. Alternatively, you can fax me on 01235 395959. Thank you.

Kind regards

Len Middlemass

comments

1. Asking someone for a favour should be a fairly straightforward process, but too many people complicate matters either by becoming coy and writing a vague and confusing letter, or by trying to barter, offering the reader something in return, which may cause offence. If you know someone well enough to ask them for a favour, and would expect them to agree to it, then this letter should be relatively simple to compose.

2. Start by stating that you are writing to request a

favour – there is nothing to be gained by being circumspect. Then explain exactly, and as briefly and as clearly as possible, what you want from them. Make it as easy as you can for them to respond, by providing your telephone and facsimile numbers, for example. End by thanking them. A plain and simple 'thank you' is often most effective.

offering a favour

Dear Mike

I was talking to Chris Brooking earlier today and he mentioned that you are having problems obtaining sales display units and accessories for next week's convention, now that Confex Services has ceased trading.

As you may know, we have a variety of display items in storage at our main office, which we use for exhibiting at the Newtown & Holdsworth exhibitions each year. We would be happy to lend these to you – without charge, of course – if you are able to collect and return them to Radbury St Edmunds.

If we can be of assistance to you, please call our Exhibition Organiser, Will Hughes, at the main office to make the necessary arrangements. His number is 01999 789789, extension 545.

Wishing you well with your convention

Best regards

Allan Worthington
Manager

comments

1. There may be occasions when you will wish to offer to do something for someone – for example, returning a favour they did for you a while ago. The difficulty here is making it clear that this is a straightforward offer of a favour, no more and no less than that. Thus, you must avoid any indication that they will be obliged to you or that you are doing this with an ulterior motive – typically, to benefit yourself in some way. Often, this is easier said than done.

2. Probably the best advice here is to keep the letter brief and direct, and as simple as you possibly can. Indicate that you believe that the reader may welcome some form of assistance, make your offer, stressing, if necessary, that it is a no-obligation favour rather than a business proposal, and suggest what they should do if they want to take you up on it. Convey the impression that you are happy to help as a matter of routine as a result of the good relations that exist between you.

reminding someone of an unfulfilled promise

Dear Justine

When we spoke last month, you were kind enough to agree to circulate copies of my curriculum vitae to your colleagues at Bristow Eves.

I sent these to you after our conversation, but have not heard anything since then. I'm not sure, therefore, whether they failed to arrive, or if the cv didn't appeal to your colleagues!

Either way, I enclose a further six copies of an amended curriculum vitae and trust that you are still happy to pass them on, as agreed. Thank you.

With best wishes

Yours sincerely

Martin Strickson

---

comments

1. This is a very difficult letter to compose, especially if someone has promised to do you a favour, but has not followed it through. If it is something important, you will wish to pursue it, but this requires considerable tact and diplomacy if you are to retain their goodwill and have the favour carried out.

2. In the opening paragraph, remind them politely of their promise. It is wise not to use the word 'promise' or anything similar, as this emphasises the favour and their failure to fulfil it, and sounds recriminatory, too.

3. The second paragraph needs to be handled with particular care, suggesting that the promise has not been kept, but without accusing or blaming the recipient, as this is the fastest way of losing their goodwill. It is sensible, whenever possible, to imply that something must have gone astray, has been overlooked due to pressure of work, heavy commitments, or whatever, rather than suggesting outright that they have forgotten, have not made the effort, and so on.

4. In the last paragraph, give them the opportunity to fulfil their promise by providing more copies of a

curriculum vitae, replacements of relevant documentation, updated information and so forth, as relevant.

5. Do be careful to check that they have not fulfilled the promise before you write, though – perhaps by contacting one of the colleagues, in the case of the example. If they have fulfilled their promise, such a letter may anger them, embarrass you and damage your relationship.

reminding someone of an unfulfilled obligation

Dear Ms Davies

<u>Account 2003</u>

We write to draw your attention to our letter of 17 May in which we agreed to accept the return of the unsold items on your Brimax stand in order to reduce the overhead balance on the above account. This was on the understanding that they would be received no later than 31 May so that they could be resold in time for the new season.

To date, we do not appear to have received these goods and must ask you to give this matter your immediate attention, to ensure that they are returned to us no later than 21 June.

If we do not receive the goods by that date, we will assume that you no longer wish to return them, and will initiate our standard procedures for recovering outstanding debts.

Yours sincerely

Dawn Race
Manager

comments

1. In some respects, this seems to be a comparable letter to the preceding one, which reminded someone of an unfulfilled promise (see page 152). However, in this instance, the reader is indebted to you rather than vice versa, so the approach may be very different. It may vary from a gentle reminder to a firm insistence, depending on how important the obligation is to you, how far they have overlooked it, what the effects will be if they continue to do so, and how much you want to remain on good terms with them.

2. The framework for an effective letter of this type is to begin by setting out what their obligation to you is – to pay a certain sum on an agreed date, to return goods, or whatever. Then suggest – or insist, according to the strength of your approach – that they have not fulfilled their obligation, and, of some importance, specify a time limit for remedying the matter. Conclude by stating what will happen if they do not do it by then – ranging from the cancellation of your agreement, to the commencement of legal action, as appropriate in your situation. Remember to follow through, though, to maintain your status and reputation.

requesting media coverage

Dear Mr Cornwell

We write to invite you to send a reporter and a photographer to cover the opening of our new Sports World store in Riseborough in a fortnight's time. This will be of particular interest to your readers in the town and its surrounding areas who currently have to travel into Foxleigh to buy sports goods and equipment.

The event will take place at 10 am on Saturday 16 July at 76 Brightwell Road, Riseborough. The store will be opened by Ipsworth footballers Alex Scowcroft and James Mathie who will be signing autographs, handing out free gifts and using the equipment until midday.

Please let me know if you will be able to send someone along – my telephone and fax numbers are 01464 230123 and 01464 234543 respectively.

I look forward to your response.

Yours sincerely

Dean King
Manager

---

comments

1. It is always worth trying to obtain media coverage for the opening of a new business, the launch of a product, service or whatever, as this will be as effective as the equivalent in advertising space. Journalists are busy, so keep the letter short and to the point. Fax it through, marked for the attention of the news editor.

2. Say what you want straight away and give them a good reason for doing it – usually this involves telling them how they will benefit from it, but in this instance you would stress that it is something that their readers (listeners or viewers) would wish to know about.

3. Provide them with the facts – when and where the event is taking place, who will be there, what they will be doing and why, as appropriate. If photographic opportunities are available for the press, all the better. Draw attention to this if necessary. Enclose a map and

directions if you feel that these would be useful – for example, they will probably be essential if a journalist from a trade magazine is coming to your premises for the first time.

4. Conclude by asking them to contact you by telephone or fax, making a point to provide them with these numbers. This will give you the chance to talk and sell the idea to them, and to supply further information, as required.

5. As journalists are so busy, you may need to follow up the letter in a week's time, perhaps with a telephone call. If they do not attend, it is still a good idea to forward key facts about the event – with transparencies, if available – shortly after it has been held. It may then receive a brief mention somewhere in the publication within the next few days.

declining a media interview

Dear Bob

Thank you for inviting me to participate in the Dave Benton Midday debate on animal testing.

Unfortunately, because of work commitments, it is not possible for me to contribute to this. As this is such an important issue, I am unable to suggest a replacement for me from within the company.

I am sorry I cannot assist you on this occasion, but hope we may have the opportunity to work together at some stage in the future.

Yours sincerely

Elsa Schugardt
Press Relations Officer

comments

1. Sometimes you will be asked to contribute to a press article, radio or television programme, putting across a viewpoint on behalf of your company. More often than not, you will be pleased to take part in order to promote your firm and its goods and services. However, occasionally you will not wish to participate – perhaps you are extremely busy, have nothing of value to say or the viewpoint is likely to be unpopular and controversial, and is not something you want to express publicly, especially in a 'live' situation when mistakes can so easily be made. In this instance, your response needs to be a diplomatic one.

2. Start by thanking them for the invitation. There is no need to make any additional comments here.

3. Next, give a bland, standardised reason for not being able to take part – previously arranged meetings, heavy work commitments, and the like. To avoid being pursued further, indicate, if necessary, that no one else from the company is able to take your place.

4. Finish by expressing regret and indicating that you hope there will be opportunities to work together in the future.

complaining about media coverage

Dear Mr Bennett

We write to complain about the incorrect comments made about the opening of our new business in the article headed 'New Store for Town' on page 12 of Thursday's edition of the *Evening Echo*.

In this article, your reporter stated that:

■ We stock baby clothes exclusively.

- We open Monday to Saturday, 9 am to 5 pm.
- Our telephone number is 01555 778788.

These statements are wrong. The facts are as follows:

- We stock exclusive baby clothes and children's wear to the age of 12 years.
- We open until 8 pm on Thursday and Friday evenings.
- Our telephone number is 01555 778778.

In addition, your reporter failed to mention that we carry a range of maternity wear, as promised during my meeting with him on 12 April.

Although we appreciate your efforts to give us coverage, it is essential that the correct facts are provided for your readers. I am sure you will realise that the details supplied on this occasion could cause us to lose potential custom.

With this in mind, we would like you to run another article about our store so that the correct information can be given to your readers. We suggest something could be written about our maternity wear, as this is the first time in many years that these goods have been available in Purdington.

We look forward to your response – telephone 01555 778778.

Yours

Janet Rhea
Co-owner

---

comments

1. This is a tricky letter to write, especially if the coverage given to your firm, goods and services was positive, but factually incorrect. To maintain goodwill and future free publicity, it is generally sensible to overlook errors unless they are likely to cause considerable embarrassment, inconvenience and/or loss of trade.

On those occasions, you need to forward a friendly but firm letter, by fax perhaps, to the editor for maximum impact.

2. Although this may be a lengthy and detailed letter – depending on the number and severity of mistakes made – the main points covered within it should be the same. Make your complaint, referring specifically to its cause. State the errors, quoting them if appropriate. Set out the correct information, with (independent) verification, if necessary. Say how you (might) have been affected adversely and indicate what you want to be done to remedy matters.

3. A good compromise can be the publication of another feature in which the correct details are given. This is always worth suggesting.

4. If you have suffered from a negative and inaccurate media report, then you (or a solicitor) will need to write a similar, but much stiffer, letter, and will want to conclude with a more forceful paragraph, perhaps including a sentence along the lines of 'We require an apology, and in the same position and with equal prominence as the original article'.

inviting someone to speak at an event

Dear Murray

I am in the process of organising our annual business-to-business communications exhibition and conference at the Grand Hotel, Myville, Humberside on 14–16 October, and wonder whether you would be interested in speaking at this event. You may recall that we discussed this possibility at last year's show, and I am now taking you up on the idea.

I would like to suggest that you make a 30-minute presentation on 'The Role of E-commerce in the Export Industry' in the main hall during the afternoon of 15 October, and be available to socialise with the other participants during the following interval of approximately 20 minutes. You should know most of these participants, as the majority will be from Schieders, Atcom and Dennisons.

I am able to offer you a fee of £150 for this, and can arrange to have you collected by car from Sandersons at 2 pm and returned there at about 5.30 pm, if you wish. I am sure we can also come to an arrangement with regard to any expenses you may incur in making this presentation.

I am pleased to enclose provisional, further information about the event for your perusal. Perhaps you will give me a call once you have had a chance to study these so that we can discuss the matter in greater detail. My telephone number is 01575 576854, extension 228. I look forward to speaking to you.

With best wishes

Yours

Frank Venables
Exhibition Organiser

---

comments

1. With this letter, you need to think very carefully about why the reader would want to speak (or participate in some other way) at your event, whatever it may be. As with your other letters, this knowledge gives you a focus and something to work towards. Ask yourself, what's in it for them. In the example, the reader is most likely to be motivated by the chance to promote their own business during their speech and to meet key players in the industry afterwards. The fee probably

will be of some significance as well, but may not be of primary concern.

2. In the first paragraph, you should provide brief, relevant details about the event – its type, purpose, participants, activities, dates and location, in particular. Bear in mind what the prospective speaker wants and needs to know about and concentrate on this information.

3. Next, tell them what you want them to do – perhaps to arrive at a certain time, speak for a set period on a specific topic and then take questions from the floor, socialise with attendees afterwards, and depart at an agreed time. Try to suggest what is in it for them too, when you write this paragraph – for example, they may be able to talk to prospective customers.

4. State what you are offering them for doing this – typically a fee, plus travel, accommodation and sundry expenses. If the fee is negotiable, say so here but indicate the figure you have in mind, which should be slightly less than you will agree to so that they can negotiate upwards.

5. Any other details can be mentioned in the final paragraph or reference can be made to accompanying literature that provides them with further information. Conclude by asking them to contact you and include your telephone number so that they can do this easily.

inviting someone to attend an event

Dear Linda

Hudson Associates are organising the Enterprise 2000 exhibition from 2 to 4 March at the Rushmore Centre, High Road East, Fettlewell, Cambridgeshire, and invite you to attend, or to send a colleague on behalf of your company, Laflin PR Ltd.

This popular annual event promises to be bigger and more exciting this year than ever before. As you will see from the enclosed brochure, over 60 exhibitors will be there, ranging from accountants through local authority employees to trade body representatives, all with a special interest in small and growing companies in this region.

During this three-day event, you will have the opportunity to meet and talk to these specialists, most of whom are offering free, 30-minute consultations to pre-registered visitors. You are also invited to attend, without charge, the hourly presentations by leading business experts such as Michael Lake and Maddie Greene, and to participate in the subsequent question-and-answer session. You can meet your fellow entrepreneurs as well at our daily business breakfasts and lunches – full details are enclosed.

This really is a 'must attend' event and we hope to see you there. Please complete the attached application form and return it to me at the above address as soon as you can – but hurry because places are limited and are being reserved on a first-come, first-served basis. To be assured of your place, please reply today.

Yours sincerely

Graham Robert
Organiser, Management Events

---

comments

1. In many ways, this is a comparable letter to the preceding one on page 161, inviting someone to speak at an event. The main difference is that you are asking the recipient of this letter to attend as part of the audience at the exhibition, conference, or whatever it is you are organising.
2. Consider why they would want to come – to learn more about the subject, to meet colleagues or even to

be seen, perhaps? Set out the key details about the event in the opening paragraph and follow this by telling them the benefits of attending – your comments should draw on their reasons for wanting to be there. Give additional facts and figures at the end or refer to the attached literature in which these can be found. Encourage a response, perhaps by indicating that places are limited, and enclose a telephone number or a coupon for their reply.

cancelling an event

Dear Mr Addison-Turner

We regret to inform you that the Excom 2000 conference scheduled for 5–6 May at the Hotel Leofric in Covendham, Wiltshire, has been cancelled.

Unfortunately, we have not received the number of firm bookings required by this stage to continue with the event. We apologise for any inconvenience this may cause to you.

We are hoping to reschedule the event for later in the year and will write to you again in due course, if this proves to be possible. Your booking documentation and deposit are being returned to you under separate cover and will be with you within the next few days.

Yours sincerely

Kerry Jordache
Events Co-ordinator

comments

1. Start by giving the main details of the event being cancelled, and provide the reason. You do need to say why the event is being cancelled. Otherwise, it seems rude and may create alarm, as the recipient wonders whether your firm has run out of money, or whatever.

2. Usually, the cause of a cancellation is that you were over-optimistic with your projections or made other misjudgements, but you will not wish to draw attention to such errors in public. However, these shortcomings will result in a lack of support for the event and most people will readily accept this as a good enough reason in itself, seeing it as 'a sign of the times', or something similar. So use this as an all-purpose reason.

3. Follow with an apology, indicate that the event may be rearranged for a later date (if relevant) and end by dealing with any practicalities such as the issue of refunds.

rejecting an invitation to an event

Dear Alice

Thank you very much indeed for inviting me to the launch of the new Desperado range at your headquarters on 25 October. It sounds as though this will be an exciting and memorable occasion.

Unfortunately, I am unable to attend as I am fully booked on that day with meetings of our conference management committee, in preparation for our Info – 2001 event at the end of next month.

I am extremely disappointed about this and trust you will update me on all the news and information about the launch in due course.

Kind regards

Nick Moffat
Sales Director

---

comments

1. Inevitably, you will be invited to various events during the course of your work, and there will be some that you do not need nor wish to attend. At the same time, you do not want to harm an existing or potential relationship and will need to reply diplomatically in such circumstances.
2. In the first paragraph, thank them for the invitation, referring to the event in positive terms – 'interesting', 'exciting', and the like.
3. The second paragraph should decline the invitation as politely as possible, and give a reason – pre-arranged meetings, a demanding workload and essential preparations for something else are all broadly acceptable, standard reasons that should not cause offence.
4. In the third paragraph, express regret at being unable, rather than unwilling, to come along, and ask to be kept up to date on all the news and information. This indicates that you really are interested in what is going on.

declining involvement in an event

Dear Patricia

Thank you for inviting us to exhibit at your forthcoming exhibition at the Grange Country Park Hotel on 28–30 June.

Unfortunately, our advertising budget is fully committed for this year so we cannot accept your invitation on this occasion.

However, we wish you every success. Please feel free to contact us again for any future events.

With best wishes

Yours sincerely

Dawn Baker
Promotions Manager

comments

1. From time to time you will be asked to advertise in a special feature planned in the press or on the radio, to exhibit at a trade fair, or to participate in an event that you do not wish to become involved with for whatever reason. In order to avoid causing offence now and to maintain good relations for the future, you need to develop a standardised response for dealing with these approaches in an appropriate manner.

2. The best reply involves thanking them for the invitation, indicating that the particular budget is used up, declining the invitation, wishing them well and

suggesting that they contact you again on future occasions (if you want them to do this). Keep it short and simple – sufficiently brief to discourage an immediate follow-up from them, but courteous enough to remain on amicable terms. You never know when you may require their assistance, so don't offend them!

announcing a retirement

Dear James

We are writing to inform you that Ashley Carpendale is retiring as our sales agent for the South East on 31 December.

Ashley has been with us at Coopers for 12 years, during which time he has become a well-known and much respected figure in the trade, not least for his courteous manner and dedication to helping customers at all times. We are sure you will miss him as much as we will do.

Norman Peters, who is currently covering our North West territory, is taking over from Ashley on 1 January and is looking forward to being of continued service to you. He will be joining Ashley on his December calls in order to get to know you and to ensure a smooth change-over in the New Year.

Meantime, if you have queries, do not hesitate to telephone Ashley on 01112 212324 or Norman on 01909 181164.

With good wishes

Yours sincerely

Barry Beardsley
Sales Director

comments

1. This is an unusual letter. Ostensibly, you are paying tribute to a retiring colleague by praising them to customers, or whoever. At the same time, you want to notify everyone that a change is taking place, it is being handled professionally, and everything will continue as smoothly as before.
2. It becomes easier to compile if you view the letter in four stages: a brief, introductory statement of who is retiring and when; a paragraph praising the person retiring and their qualities; another paragraph explaining who is taking over, how and when; and a final statement inviting the recipient to call for further information.

announcing a death

Dear Miss Chatfield

It is with the deepest regret that I write to tell you of the death of June Baxendale. June was a dear friend and a stalwart of the company. I know she was greatly respected by everyone in the industry.

For the time being, Janice McManaman is taking care of June's work and we would be grateful if any enquiries could be directed to her.

June's funeral is to be held at 2.30 on 17 April at Worthington Crematorium should you wish to come along. Flowers should be sent to Pennington's Funeral Directors at 26 Windmill Road, Rustingside, Essex RT45 7FP.

Yours sincerely

David Leach
Director

comments

1. In many respects, this is a similar letter to the one announcing retirement on page 168, but requiring greater tact and diplomacy.
2. To begin with, you should tell the reader of your colleague's death and pay a simple but sincere tribute to them. Personalise this by using 'I' rather than 'we'.
3. You need to indicate that someone is taking care of the deceased person's workload as you do not wish to lose any business. Do this discreetly, almost dismissively, to avoid causing offence.
4. At the end of the letter, give details of the funeral and other relevant arrangements in case the recipient wishes to attend, send flowers, or whatever.
5. Writing about someone's death is always difficult, especially if you were close to them. Often, there is much you want to say, but are unable to find the right words to express yourself. Simplicity is the key to success – 'June was a dear friend' conveys far more than a garbled and possibly incoherent description of what she was like.
6. A week or two after the funeral, a follow-up letter can be sent, outlining the way in which the department or firm has been re-organised for the future.